# THE JAMES M. CAIN

# THE JAMES M. CAIN COOKBOOK

*GUIDE TO HOME SINGING,*
*PHYSICAL FITNESS, AND*
*ANIMALS (ESPECIALLY CATS)*

EDITED BY
ROY HOOPES AND
LYNNE BARRETT

CARNEGIE MELLON UNIVERSITY PRESS
PITTSBURGH 1988

Library of Congress Catalog Card Number 86–72296

ISBN 0–88748–046–2

ISBN 0–88748–047–0  Pbk.

# CONTENTS

Most people associate James M. Cain with his novels of murder and adultery (*The Postman Always Rings Twice; Double Indemnity*), prostitution (*Past All Dishonor*), homosexuality (*Serenade*), and incest (*The Butterfly*). But less well known is the fact that Cain started his career as a human-interest editorial writer, working for Walter Lippmann on *The New York World*, and that long after the surprising success of *The Postman* in 1934 stamped him forever as a "tough-guy writer," he remained preoccupied with the subjects he dealt with as a human-interest editorial writer. Cain learned early in his career what people were really interested in, and, next to sex, he decided food, animals and opera singers were the subjects which fascinated people the most. They were also his interests, as will be seen from these essays and stories that span his entire 60 years as a journalist and storyteller.

Roy Hoopes

# I

COOKBOOK

"*What are you having tonight?*"

"*Who says I'm having anything?*"

"*Now listen, have we got to go all over that? Baby, baby, you go out with him, and he buys you a dinner, and you get a little tight, and you come home, and something happens, and then what?*"

"*Don't worry. Nothing'll happen.*"

"*Oh something'll happen. If not tonight, then some other night. Because if it don't happen, he'll lose interest, and quit coming around, and you wouldn't like that. And when it happens, it's Sin. It's Sin, because you're a grass widow, and fast. And he's all paid up, because he bought your dinner, and that makes it square.*"

"*He must have a wonderful character, my Wally.*"

"*He's got the same character they've all got, no better and no worse. But—if you bought his dinner, and cooked it for him the way only you can cook, and you just happened to look cute in that little apron, and something just happened to happen, then it's Nature. Old Mother Nature, baby, and we all know she's no bum. Because that grass widow, she went back to the kitchen, where all women belong, and that makes it all right. And Wally, he's not paid up, even a little bit. He even forgot to ask the price of the chips. He'll find out. And another thing, this way is quick, and the last I heard of you, you were up against it, and couldn't afford to waste much time. You play it right and inside of a week your financial situation will be greatly eased, and inside of a month you'll have him begging for the chance to buy that divorce. The other way, making the grand tour of all the speako's he knows, it could go on for five years, and even then you couldn't be sure.*"

"*You think I want to be kept?*"

"*Yes.*"

*For a while after that, Mildred didn't think of Wally, at any rate to know she was thinking of him . . .*

*. . . But around four o'clock, when it started to rain, she put the sewing basket away, went to the kitchen, and checked her supplies from the three or four oranges in reserve for the children's breakfast to the vegetables she had bought yesterday in the market. The chicken she gave a good smelling, to make sure it was still fresh. The quart of milk she took out of the icebox with care, so as not to joggle it, and, using a tiny ladle intended for salt, removed the thick cream at the top and put it into a glass pitcher. Then she opened a can of huckleberries and made a pie. While that was baking she stuffed the chicken.*

from *Mildred Pierce*

# INTRODUCTION

 he year was 1934 and the ex-newspaperman and unsuccessful Hollywood screenwriter, James M. Cain, had, almost overnight, become the most controversial author in the country. The book which propelled him out of obscurity into the mainstream of popular fiction was *The Postman Always Rings Twice,* a novel about lust, adultery and murder which not only rocked readers and critics but shook the publishing world, which naturally wanted more. Alfred A. Knopf, his publisher, was urging Cain to write another novel and his agent, Edith Haggard in New York, was pleading with him to write a magazine serial or some short stories—preferably about murder, adultery, or any subject that would be suitable for the much-discussed, hard boiled prose of James M. Cain. Already he was being called a "tough guy" writer.

In Hollywood, Cain was working furiously—mostly on "treatments" for screenplays (which came back from the studios almost as fast as he could send them in), his syndicated Hearst column and an idea for a series of articles on what was really his favorite subject. He sent the first—on how to carve a turkey—to Mrs. Haggard and an outline for more articles on Midnight Spaghetti, Crepes Suzette, Christmas Eggnog, a Wild Duck Dinner, The Mint Julep, etc. Mrs. Haggard could not believe it. "With the magazine world at your feet," she replied, desperately, "with their hands raised high over their heads pleading with you for short stories, you want to write food articles. Please," she pleaded, "for the little widow, do a story. I just know the winter will be long and hard."

Cain responded with two more food articles, but did agree to think about a magazine serial—which he eventually wrote. When it was published two years later, in *Liberty*, it created almost as much of a sensation as *The Postman*. Its title, of couse, was *Double Indemnity*. And Mrs. Haggard sold three of his food articles to *Esquire*, which pleased Cain very much.

He had first become intrigued with the subject of food when he was writing editorials for the *New York World*. "The perennial, never-fail, always good for a ha-ha subject of subjects," he said, was something about eating. An editorial on food—the great "pepper upper" of the letters column—never failed to bring an avalanche of responses from readers. This discovery came with an editorial on what he soon found was a national institution—and which, for the record, is reprinted in its entirety from the July 14, 1925, *New York World:*

# Huckleberry Pie

The pie season is here. All those things of which pie is made can be had fresh and cheap. Which brings to mind a neglected public issue—the deterioration of huckleberry pie. Here is a blot on the national escutcheon. Huckleberry pie, as originally invented, was essentially poetical; it contained that lyric quality which marks off poetry from the utile arts: it exalted the soul, lifted us for a moment from the earth to the stars. There was but one way to make it. The crust was thin and flaky. The berries were used in their natural state. Thus, when the pie was baked, great quantities of juice stewed out, staining the crust a rich purple. Service was in soup-plates. Cream was added until, in juice and cream combined, the pie floated. The diner was allowed a spoon, fork, ladle or whatever he required, and was not debarred from tying his napkin back of his ears. When huckleberrry pie came on the table, regular rules were suspended in the interest of art.

Now all is changed. Huckleberry pie has come under the pie-baking trust. The crust is no longer thin, but thick; the berries have cornstarch added to them, so the juice curdles into a pasty jelly. No longer is service in soup-plates, and no longer do we add cream. The dark purple blobs on the crust are a thing of the past. How long shall we stand this outrage? The modern technique may facilitate the delivery of pie in stacks, but it has driven a dirk into the heart of poetry. If we are free men, not slaves, let us rise and demand our rights.

Rise they did, like a great souffle, and the *World* editorial offices were deluged with letters from unhappy huckleberry pie lovers. A city-wide crisis had been ignited, and eleven days later, Cain followed with this editorial:

## The Pie Rebellion Grows

We note with gratification that the Rotary Club has met the huckleberry-pie issue fairly and squarely. It is only by concerted effort that we can save this deplorable situation and bring back huckleberry pie as executed by the founders of our Republic and embodied in the highest law of the land. It is to be regretted that a speaker cited caloric values. This only results in beclouding the issue. That issue is not whether huckleberry pie is digestible or not, but whether we, as free American citizens, are going to have pie as it was and by right ought to be, or whether we are going to submit to a base imitation thickened up with corn-starch, not fit for serfs and peons to eat. And for that matter, which is the more digestible—huckleberry pie as we knew it or this new abomination?

We are glad to report a ray of hope. A pie arriving since publication of our first editorial on the subject upholds in all respects the best American tradition. The species, at least, is not yet extinct. Let us work together to bring back huckleberry pie as we used to have it, as mother used to make it, and as Washington, Jefferson and Benjamin Franklin used to eat it.

*New York World,* July 25, 1925

This crisis was finally resolved—but not until the President of Schraff's sent over to the *World's* "pie editor" two of its huckleberry pies as proof that his company made its pies with free-running juices.

Soon thereafter, a new crisis emerged—mostly in the *World's* City Room. In another editorial, Cain had raised the question of whether big or little frog legs were preferred by gourmets and commented that the biggest legs he had ever seen were from West Virginia. This prompted one reader from Virginia to write in claiming that Old Dominion frog legs were the biggest in the world and that, furthermore, he could prove it—which he did, by sending a box of Virginia's finest to *The World*. By mistake they landed up in the City Room where the editor opened them and soon huge—maybe even the world's largest—frogs were jumping off typewriters and onto desks, prompting more than one hung-over reporter to go on the wagon for awhile. Cain, of course, became the "frog editor."

Then he became the "hog editor" when he wrote an editorial about hog calling, in which he asked "for what conceivable reason would anyone ever call hogs?" He soon found out: every editorial writer on a non-metropolitan paper in the country took it upon himself to set the ignorant New York writer straight and the *Literary Digest* considered the controversy of such national import that it devoted two pages to it. But after all the rural editorial pages had printed their hog calls, Cain noted that no two calls were alike, so he rushed into print with an anthology of hog calls, noting their differences, and said that if the experts themselves could not agree on what a hog call sounded like, it was presumptuous for a New York City fellow even to have an opinion. Finally, one day, Lippmann came striding into the editorial office and said, "I'm sick of these goddamn hogs."

The hog-calling gambit was over, but by now Cain had learned his lesson: the average reader was fascinated by anything to do with food. In fact, *The World* conducted a poll to determine just what America's favorite food was and Cain speculated, in an editorial, what election night in the News Room would be like—"the reporters sitting nervously at their desks, the city editor dashing about, placards on each desk to show who is tabulating which, placards like Onions, Fried Chicken, Maryland Turkey, Ham and Eggs, and Sirloin Steak, Family Style. Then, as the zero hour draws near, picture the city editor mounted on a stool, seizing bulletins as the messengers appear, and howling: 'Harlem gives 5,364 for ICE COLD WATERMELON,' 'Greenwich Village piles up 8,693 for CINNAMON TOAST.'

"And then, outside, what a scene as the crowds gather to watch the bulletins flashed on the screen across the street. Think of the cheers as the lead alternates between Corned Beef and Ham. And then, when Ham finally wins, the demonstration. And when the Committee on Notification finally calls on Ham to tell him of the great victory no doubt Ham will say: 'I was a live pig once. Why did you wait until after the funeral to do me this honor?'"

Cain continued writing editorials on food (a few of which are reprinted here) until *The World* folded in 1931. Then, when he was in Hollywood, he briefly wrote a by-lined, syndicated column for Hearst, which proved another outlet for his favorite subject. While writing the Hearst column, he continued his campaigns (begun while he was on *The World*) to make muskrat and catfish, if not national, at least popular, dishes. And after he had written a couple of columns on the catfish, Cain went East where he visited one of his favorite New York restaurants, Moneta's. Cain recalls that Mr. Moneta came running up to him "in high excitement, waving a menu at me. It carried a dish—'Tuce a la Cain.' He said it was quite a hit. 'Sell'm all a time, sell'm big. Call'm catfish, no sell at all. Call'm tuce a la Cain, sell'm big."

As do most novelists, Cain preferred to write about subjects he knew something about, hence singing and food (especially the preparation of it) was given perhaps as much attention as sex and crime—well almost. One of Cain's most successful nonviolent novels—*Career in C-Major*—is about a man who learns that he can sing better than his wife, who is an opera star. He once had a similar idea for a book about a cook—which he outlined to a friend: "A man has the illusion he's a better cook than his wife, and sometimes is able to prove it by some tour de force in the kitchen, forgetting that his grand performances are always special programs, done once to great applause, and not repeated until next time. Her programs, however, are done 21 times a week, in fair weather or foul, and by that very fact, entitled to appraisal on a different basis from the bar-b-que job in the garden. However, it didn't seem to fizz."

But it is no accident that, just as in *Double Indemnity* the principal character is an insurance agent (which Cain had once been, in addition to which he had learned much about the business from his father) and in *Serenade* the principal character is an opera star (which Cain had once hoped to be himself and had studied briefly for a singing career), in *Postman* and *Mildred Pierce,* the principal characters operate restaurants. Cain was always fascinated by restaurants and in his early days ate many dinners in them because of a disintegrating first marriage and, in his second marriage, a wife who spent most of their first two married years in Finland settling business affairs. "I took to dining at Lee Chumley's around the corner (from the gold-domed *World* building on Park Row) and he would sit down for a chat—but chats with a restaurant keeper wind up the same way: a waitress appears with an unhappy look on her face and he excuses himself and goes."

Cain continued his interest in restaurants after he went to California and, according to his son-in-law Leo Tysencki, in 1932 he struck up an acquaintance with the maitre d' at the Townhouse restaurant. His name was Alexander Perino, and he wanted to start his own restaurant, which Cain encouraged. Perino's soon became a landmark on Wilshire Boulevard and a place for the stars to see and be seen. A 1958 article in *Holiday* by Eugene Burdick shows a full page photograph of Perino posed "with friends, Mr. and Mrs. Ronald Reagan," as the caption put it. Cain continued his friendship with Perino and the restaurateur often came by the Cain home on Belden Drive, where he instructed "Jamie," as Leo Tysencki says his friend called Cain, in the fine art of spaghetti fixing.

Cain himself then became something of an expert on the preparation of spaghetti dinners, which he served at the famous Cain home sing-ins (see next section) he staged in the 1930s for Hollywood friends who shared his interest in music. Spaghetti was, in fact, the perfect dinner for such occasions. Cain spent considerable time cooking, although he always insisted that he was not a good cook and spent most of his time in the kitchen so he could write knowledgeably about food. And as an ex-reporter and editorial writer, he insisted that his books be exhaustively researched. "Every year, you have 800 stinking books by evening meal writers," he once told an interviewer, "who betray their ignorance by writing, in say, a book about Mexico: 'The family sat down to their evening meal.' Too damned lazy even to get out and go downtown to the Mexican consulate, find a secretary and ask questions."

In his novels, he preferred to concentrate on the serving of the dinner, the ambiance, the wines, etc., as if he were a frustrated proprietor of a restaurant, which he probably was. But his best writing on food came in the articles which Mrs. Haggard sold to *Esquire* (and are reprinted here) in the mid-1930s. The first article was on carving the turkey and there is an odd little footnote to this essay. When I researched my biography of Cain, one of his early friends I wrote for information was E. B. White, who worked with Cain on the *New Yorker*. White graciously responded from his Maine retreat, saying that, among other things, he remembered Cain entertaining them one Thanksgiving day "with a turkey dinner and a new marriage. The turkey was bigger than the platter and Jim delivered a monologue as he carved, while the slices of meat slipped quietly to the floor."

James M. Cain maintained his interest in food to the end of his life and in his twilight years, when he wrote a few articles for the *Washington Post* magazine, he included one little gem of an essay on the mint julep. The truth is, Cain liked to approach *haute cuisine* with a little low humor and bring the whole business down into the mean streets where he and his literary colleagues, Raymond Chandler and Dashiell Hammett, felt more comfortable. Although Tuce Fish a la Cain created something of a stir in New York in 1934, Cain's most famous dish was the Iguana soup shared by John Sharp, the down and out opera singer, and Juana, the Mexican whore who befriended Sharp and helped him regain his voice. They ate the soup in *Serenade,* probably the most controversial novel published in the 1930s, with Sharp speaking its famous opening line: "I was in the Tupinamba, having a bizocho and coffee, when this girl came in." The girl was Juana and soon a thunderstorm would drive them into a church where they would make love in front of the altar and then fix some Iguana soup. The rest is culinary history.

# D R I N K

□□□□□□□□□□□□□□□□□□□□□□□□

## *Repeal*

"*B*aby, what are you doing about Repeal?"

"*You mean Repeal of Prohibition?*"

"*Yeah, just that.*"

"*Why, I don't see how it affects me.*"

"*It affects you plenty.*"

Mrs. Gessler, having coffee with Mildred just before closing time, began to talk very rapidly. Repeal, she said, was only a matter of weeks, and it was going to stand the whole restaurant business on its head. "*People are just crazy for a drink, a decent drink, a drink with no smoke or ether or formaldehyde in it, a drink they can have out in the open, without having to give the password to some yegg with his face in a slot. And places that can read the handwriting on the wall are going to cash in, and those that can't are going to pass out. You think you've got a nice trade here, don't you? And you think it'll stick by you, because it likes you, and likes your chicken, and wants to help a plucky little woman get along? It will like hell. When they find out you're not going to serve them that drink, they're going to be sore and stay sore. They're going to tag you for a back number and go some place where they get what they want. You're going to be out of luck.*"

"*You mean I should sell* liquor?"

"*It'll be legal, won't it?*"

"*I wouldn't even consider such a thing.*"

"*Why not?*"

*"Do you think I'd run a* saloon?"

*Mrs. Gessler lit a cigarette, began snapping the ashes impatiently into Mildred's Mexican ashtrays. Then she took Mildred to task for prejudice, for stupidity, for not being up with the times. Mildred, annoyed at being told how to run her business, argued back, but for each point she made Mrs. Gessler made two points. She kept reminding Mildred that liquor, when it came back, wasn't going to be the same as it had been in the old days. It was going to be respectable, and it was going to put the restaurant business on its feet. "That's what has ailed eating houses ever since the war. That's why you're lucky to get a lousy 85 cents for your dinner, when if you could sell a drink with it, you could get a buck, and maybe a buck and a quarter. Baby, you're not talking sense, and I'm getting damned annoyed at you."*

*"But I don't know anything about liquor."*

*"I do."*

from *Mildred Pierce*


# Tasting Liquor
## Why the Bootlegger's Bill
## Is Larger Than It Need Be


One of the curious revelations brought about by prohibition is the almost complete lack of capacity on the part of Americans for anything describable as gustatory connoisseurship.

Here is a law, remember, that threw into the discard all ordinary standards of quality in products, as well as all ordinary safeguards to the consumer. Trademarks it rendered useless, for it put a premium on forgery, at the same time providing no penalities for forgery. The commercial conscience of the vender it did away with completely, for it drew into trade persons who have no commercial conscience. Prosecutions for fraud it rendered impossible, for it proclaimed liquor an outlaw commodity, with no standing in court whatever. Thus it brought on a state of affairs in which the consumer was quite on his own. He was in the same position as a buyer for a cigar factory among the piles of leaf down in Danville, or a tea importer on the arrival of a shipment from Formosa, or a tailor confronted with new bolts of cloth. He had to judge the product on its merits, knowing that any representations about it were as worthless as a trader's representations about a horse. But have the American people learned to do this, or even begun to learn it? Not so far as I have been able to make out. I know a number of persons who do quite a little drinking, or at any rate quite a lot of talking about drinking. They tell tall tales about the cocktails on 58th Street, the beer in Hoboken, and the wine on Bleecker Street. But there is not one of them who can pour a small glass of whisky, taste it, and return a plain "yes" or "no." I know they cannot do this by the look in their eye, by their hemming and hawing, by the great amount of gabbling that precedes what they call their verdicts. They simply haven't the manner of experts. And I know they cannot do it by the unfortunate misinformation they betray whenever they try it.

For example, to determine the age of whisky, they commonly pour a few drops into water and watch for the curling streaks that are supposed to show the "oiliness" of age. Or to determine the excellence of beer, they pay great attention to the depth of the collar. Now it happens that the curling streaks have nothing to do with the age of whisky. New whisky, even if it is caught as it runs out of the still, will show the same curling streaks as soon as it comes into contact with water. And it happens too that the depth of the collar has nothing to do with the merits of beer. The most villainous needle beer, if it is highly charged, or from a fresh keg, or slightly warm, will show a collar to equal that of the finest Pilsner. But these lamentable facts still do not represent the real objection to these tests, and all others like them. They dodge the whole issue: they are in the eye instead of the mouth. Even if they were valid, which they are not, they would cease to be valid as soon as the bootlegger found a way to beat them, and we should be as far as ever from the main points, which are the age of the whisky and the quality of the beer. Americans, after ten years with a problem that has only one solution, have found no way to deal with it except to trust their bootlegger, that soul of honor.

Now it seems to be fairly easy to acquire a taste, which is to say the ability to tell whether a thing is what it purports to be. In my time I have known people who had taste in things so disparate as oysters, lace, paintings and fiddles. They never pretended that it was any great trick, but this much it obviously required: a passion for the subject, a conviction that the difference between one oyster and another oyster, or between hand lace and machine lace, or between original paintings and reproductions, or between Cremona fiddles and factory fiddles, really matters. It is this passion, this interest in quality, which Americans seem unable to bring to their drink, or for that matter, to their food. Their attitude reminds me of that taken by some people toward music. "I like a concert," they say. "I find it rests me, gets my mind off my work." In other words, music to them is a sort of glorified aspirin tablet, and it is not surprising that they say some appalling things about it. The mark of a great singer, they often proclaim, is the clearness of his enunciation. It is the mark of a great singer, and it is also the mark of a great many hams: actually it proves nothing, has as little to do with the ethos of song as the collar with the ethos of beer. One sees the same lack of ability to tackle a subject in the only place that really matters, the same inclination to give weight to trivial and extraneous things, the same vulnerability to the imitation instead of the real.

Americans, I think, regard what goes into their stomachs as fuel, and as nothing else. If somebody tells them that spinach will make it burn hotter, they mix spinach with it, and if somebody tells them that cognac will make it burn brighter, they give it shot of cognac. That they ever regard it an an aesthetic achievement in its own right, as something to be enjoyed for its own sake, is most doubtful. So long as that remains true, they will be unable to appraise it critically, and their bootleggers will be able to fool them with pretty labels and stories about a friend on one of the boats.

*New York World* column
January 4, 1931

# Spirits

As my contribution to the Bicentennial Year, I shall tell how to make a mint julep, so when the gong goes bong at noon on July 4, and our third century makes its appearance, you can welcome it in with a 100 percent American drink, suitable to the occasion. I am aware, of course, that you know how to make a julep, or think you do, and that all your friends do too, so you wrangle among yourselves over various fine points of doctrine, such as how much sugar to use and whether to crush the mint or not crush it. Nevertheless, I shall tell how to make a mint julep, as I have a qualification that sets me apart from other commentators: I put first things first, as you and your friends probably don't—as indeed, nobody else does, at least as I've heard so far. And first of all, with a julep, is this basic principle: It must be pleasing to the eye. If it please the eye, other things, such as taste, will follow along automatically. But if it disappoint the eye, if it be merely a sick, sad-looking travesty of a julep, it will taste horrible too.

So what pleases the eye on a julep? Frost, mainly. A julep without frost is an egg without salt, a queer, halfway thing that makes you uncomfortable to look at, as well as to drink, or try to drink. And how do you get this frost that a julep must have? With booze, my friend— good old mountain dew, or if you serve booze aged in wood, that distinguished Blue Grass Bourbon. It takes twice as much booze to frost a julep as it does to make a julep that doesn't frost, that sad, sick kind that most people put out.

Booze, and shaved ice.

My acquaintance with shaved ice goes back a great many years, to the time, in Annapolis where I spent my boyhood, when I was six years old. One night my father had an errand at the foot of Main Street, and took me with him. It must have been Saturday night, as the market Annapolis had then was going full blast, with crowds of people in it, and pitch men off at one side, selling their wares. One of these offered snowballs. Under his flaring torch he had a machine, with a wheel on one side that had a handle on it, a door in its front, and a pea green color over all. He would crank the wheel with the handle, then open the door, and reveal a heaping cone of snow, which he would take out and squirt with a bottle, so beautiful syrup popped out on the snow. This "snowball," as he called it, he sold for one cent, which didn't seem much, and I pleaded for one to taste. I thought this crimson snowball the most beautiful thing I'd ever seen in my life. To my utter astonishment, my father said no, in no uncertain tones—he bought me popcorn for five cents, but this snowball he wouldn't even consider. For the first time I heard the word microbe, and next day looked it up in the dictionary. It was all horribly bewildering, but I still feel the disappointment, recalling that night now, that I felt as I stared at this snowball I couldn't have.

So, time lapse forty years, to Another Part of the Forest, Los Angeles, where I'm in a restaurant supply house, buying a special kinfe I wanted, to carve roast beef with. But as the knife was being wrapped up, what do I see, looking at me from a shelf, but that same snowball machine, with wheel at one side, door in the front, and a pea green coat of paint. I bought it at once and came home with it, so excited I could hardly talk. When Annalisa Guld saw it, she was excited too. She was our very pretty Swedish maid, who was a close personal friend and had often heard my sad story of the snowball I didn't get, and knew at once what it meant to me, this thing that I had brought home. No one was home except her, when I handed it over, and I went in the sitting room to unwrap my knife and examine it. Annalisa had said "I wash," when she took charge of the machine, but then appeared at the sitting room door, made her Swedish knix, and announced: "Snowball est servi."

"What? So soon?"

"You shall see—please come to the dining room."

So I went to the dining room, sat down at the table, and waited. Then sure enough here came Annalisa with the same conical plate of snow as the man had produced in Annapolis, and a bottle of strawberry syrup, with a squirt cork in it that she had dug up somewhere. She squirted the syrup on, then sat down at my invitation to see how the thing turned out. "If is terrible," she whispered, "I shall not tell. It shall be our secret, together."

Of course it was God-awful.

It reminded me of those mixes we kids used to make, by spooning snow from the window sill, adding coconut and sugar, and then trying to persuade ourselves it was good. So, the grand drink was a flop, but true to her promise, Annalisa protected me, so I didn't become the object of household derision. Still, there the machine was, and I wouldn't have been human if I didn't try to think of something to do with it. But what? By idle chance one night, a guest asked if before he went home, he could gather some mint from my mint bed. "I got a mint bed?" I answered. "Like where, for instance?"

"Like alongside your front door."

I went and looked, and sure enough there was mint, a beautiful patch of it, within a few feet of the door, the first I had known about it. So I gave him his mint, but then suddenly thought: "That can be it! That can be what I do with that thing! I can make juleps with it."

At that time, I knew nothing of how to make juleps, but learned soon enough, and with Annalisa digging up glasses, tall narrow ones that she found, and coasters, I was on my way. But my juleps weren't really good. They looked like, and from all I heard, tasted like other juleps I'd seen, but that was faint praise indeed. It seemed to me a julep should frost—and then one night, a guest's julep did. When I wanted to know why, and pressed him for what he had done to it, he went vague at once, as though denying guilt. But his wife Judas-goated on him. "He put more liquor in," she revealed, a bit waspishly. "What you gave him wasn't enough."

A great white light dawned.

I found out how to frost a julep.

You put more liquor in.

So now, I knew how to make a julep, and that might be the end of the tale, except that there's more, and I think you should know what it is, so you don't make the mistake I did, and overreach yourself, in excess of zeal. In Hollywood, and perhaps in other places, each had his own specialty—I knew one hostess whose thing was smoked oysters, another who favored sloe gin rickeys, and one Beverly Hills plutocrat who served terrapin stew at dinner, in the days when the terrapin could be had from the Isle of Good Hope Terrapin Farm, down near Savannah, Georgia. And if my specialty now would be juleps, which I thought a nice idea, I felt I should do it big, in some kind of elegant style. So, being in Baltimore one Christmas holiday visiting my parents, I looked up a silversmith that I knew, and asked how much goblets would cost, sterling goblets, with a mint leaf bumped out on their front. He quoted a price that was stiff, but in those days of motion picture salaries, one that I could afford. But the goblets he showed me I thought looked a bit small, and I asked if two inches more of silver could be soldered on to the top, to make a really impressive container. No trouble, he said—he would simply order it done.

So, in due course here come the goblets, great, big beautiful goblets, with the mint leaf giving the idea, handles, and "sterling" on the bottom. I tell you, when I made that first julep with them, it was quite a thing to see—the green mint, the white frost, the gleaming silver all combining to please the eye. "Quite a production," said one of the guests, as I appeared with a dozen silver juleps on a silver tray.

A half hour later he passed out.

They all passed out, or nearly did.

My goblets, it seemed were so big, and I had to use so much liquor to frost them, that I had defeated my own purpose. I used them that time, but no more. So, I tell of this mistake to warn you: If booze is the trick with a julep, you must use discretion—or else. So, to make juleps you must:

1. Buy, borrow, or steal a snowball machine. They can be bought at restaurant supply houses, not often at hardware stores, and you may have to scrabble around. But if you want to make juleps, a snowball machine is necessary, and there is no substitute.

2. Glasses of a certain kind you must have, too. My goblets, when at last I got around to measuring them, held twenty ounces of fluid, too much by half. The department stores sell glass goblets, with handles on them, that hold ten ounces of fluid, and these are perfect. You must have glasses with handles, else coasters that fit your straight glasses, for if the julep frosts, you can't handle it with your fingers.

3. You'll need straws, and I recommend stiff ones, not the ones that crumple as soon as they're handled. The ones I have are called Slipsticks, and they are so stiff I also use them in old fashioneds, in lieu of glass muddlers.

4. Mint, and plenty of it. You'll need about six full sprigs to each julep, and each sprig should be clipped with the scissors, until it's exactly the right length—long enough to touch the bottom of your glass, with four or five leaves sticking up over the edge—but not long enough to stand three or four inches over the edge, for reasons I'll explain.

So, as to how to proceed: Into each glass put a half teaspoonful of sugar, and a half teaspoonful of water. Strip the leaves off two sprigs of mint, and drop them into each glass. Then with a long spoon cut them up, so the mint flavor gets into the sugar. Then strip the leaves from one sprig of mint, wet them under the spigot, and with your fingers stick them to the inside of the glass, shiny side out. This is more of what appeals to the eye. Then, with your kitchen measuring cup, dole one ounce of bourbon into each glass. Then, spoon snow from your machine on top of it. Spoon snow in within an inch of the top of each glass. You can give a stir, but not too much of a stir, to the liquor under this snow. Then, again with your measuring cup, pour one more ounce of bourbon, on top of the snow now in the glass. Don't stir this. Then, with your spoon, add snow to the top for garnish.

That's your julep.

Make it a half hour before the guests get there, so it sits that long, to frost. It will frost, if you haven't skimped the bourbon, don't worry. When you're ready to serve put a straw into each glass, a quarter-circle around from the handle. The mint goes in last, two sprigs should be enough. It goes in opposite to the straw, so the guest has it under his nose as he drinks.

You will be left with one sprig of mint to each glass, and this you will need to freshen your julep, halfway along the line. A julep, delightful to the eye at first, rapidly loses appearance, as the contents of the glass are drunk, and as the mint wilts. The liquor wilts it so fast it is really discouraging. So be ready, once the julep's half drunk, to go around to each guest, pick the old mint out of his glass, stick this other sprig in, and make a joke of some kind. Encouraged this way, a julep will still look like something, clear to the end.

And, made this way, it tastes fine—or at least so my guests assure me. I don't drink myself, and though I've made 1000 juleps, I've never tasted one.

*The Washington Post*
May 9, 1976

# SOUPS & STEWS

□□□□□□□□□□□□□□□□□□□□□□□

## *The Soup of the Iguana*

*S**he wriggled into my arms, and next thing I knew it was daylight, and
she was still there. She opened her eyes, closed them again, and came
closer. Of course there wasn't but one thing to do about that, so I did it.
Next time I woke up I knew it must be late, because I was hungry as hell.*

*It rained all that day, and the next. We split up on the cooking
after the first breakfast. I did the eggs and she did the tortillas, and
that seemed to work better. I got the pot to boil at last by setting it
right on the tiles without any plate, and it not only made it boil, but
saved time. In between, though, there wasn't much to do, so we did
whatever appealed to us.*

*The afternoon of the second day it let up for about a half hour,
and we slid down in the mud to have a look at the arroyo. It was a
torrent. No chance of making Acapulco that night. We went up the hill
and the sun came out plenty hot. When we got to the church the rocks
back of it were alive with lizards. There was every size lizard you could
think of, from little ones that were transparent like shrimps, to big
ones three feet long. They were a kind of a blue gray, and moved so
fast you could hardly follow them with your eyes. They leveled out with
their tail, somehow, so they went over the rocks in a straight line, and
almost seemed to fly. Looking at them you could believe it all right,
that they turned into birds just by letting their scales grow into feathers.
You could almost believe it that they were half bird already.*

*We climbed down and stood looking at them, when all of a sudden she began to scream. "Iguana! Iguana! Look, look, big iguana!"*

*I looked, and couldn't see anything. Then, still as the rock it was lying on, and just about the color of it, I saw the evilest-looking thing I ever laid eyes on. It looked like some prehistoric monster you see in the encyclopedia, between two and three feet long, with a scruff of spines that started at its head and went clear down its back, and a look in its eye like something in a nightmare. She had grabbed up a little tree that had washed out by the roots, and was closing in on him. "What are you doing? Let that goddam thing alone!"*

*When I spoke he shot out for the next rock like something on springs, but she made a swipe and caught him in mid-air. He landed about ten feet away, with his yellow belly showing and all four legs churning him around in circles. She scrambled over, hit him again, and then she grabbed him. "Machete! Quick, bring machete!"*

*"Machete, hell, let him go I tell you!"*

*"Is iguana! We cook! We eat!"*

*"Eat!—that thing?"*

*"The machete, the machete!"*

*He was scratching her by that time, and if she wouldn't let him go I wasn't letting him make hash out of her. I dove in the church for the machete. But then some memory of this animal caught me. I don't know whether it was something I had read in Cortés, or Diaz, or Martyr, or somebody, about how they cooked it when the Aztecs still ran Mexico, or some instinct I had brought away from Paris, or what. All I knew was that if we ever cut his head off he was going to be dead, and maybe that wouldn't be right. I didn't grab a machete. I grabbed a basket, with a top on it, and dug out there with it. "The machete! The machete, give me the machete!"*

*He had come to by now, and was fighting all he knew, but I grabbed him. The only place to grab him was in the belly, on account of those spines on his back, and that put his claws right up your arm. She was bleeding up to her elbows, and now it was my turn. Never mind how he felt and how he stunk. It was enough to turn your stomach. But I gave him the squeeze, shoved him head-down in the basket, and clapped the top on. Then I held it tight with both hands.*

*"Get some twine."*

*"But the machete! Why no bring—"*

*"Never mind. I'm doing this. Twine—string—that the things were tied with."*

*I carried him in, and she got some twine, and I tied the top on, tight. Then I set him down and tried to think. She didn't make any sense out of it, but she let me alone. In a minute I fed up the fire, took the pot out and filled it with water. It had started to rain again. I came in and put the pot on to heat. It took a long while. Inside the basket those claws were ripping at the wicker, and I wondered if it would hold.*

*At last I got a simmer, and then I took the pot off and got another basket-top ready. I picked him up, held him way above my head, and dropped him to the floor. I remembered what shock did to him the first time, and I hoped it would work again. It didn't. When I cut the string and grabbed, I got teeth, but I held on and socked him in the pot. I whipped the basket-top on and held it with my knee. For three seconds it was like I had dropped an electric fan in there, but then it stopped. I took the top off and fished him out. He was dead, or as dead as a reptile ever gets. Then I found out why it was that something had told me to put him in the pot alive, and not cook him dead, with his head cut off, like she wanted to do. When he hit that scalding water he let go. He purged, and that meant he was clean inside as a whistle.*

*I went out, emptied the pot, heated a little more water, and scrubbed it clean with cornhusks, from the eggs. Then I scrubbed him off. Then I filled the pot, or about two thirds filled it, with clean water, and put it on the fire. When it began to smoke I dropped him in.* "But is very fonny. Mamma no cook that way."

"Is fonny, but inspiration has hit me. Never mind how Mamma does it. This is how I do it, and I think it's going to be good."

*I fed up the fire, and pretty soon it boiled. I cut it down to a simmer, and this smell began to come off it. It was a stink, and yet it smelled right, like I knew it was going to smell. I let it cook along, and every now and then I'd fish him up and pull one of his claws. When a claw pulled out I figured he was done. I took him out and put him in a bowl. She reached for the pot to go out and empty it. I almost fainted.* "Let that water alone. Leave it there, right where it is."

*I cut off his head, opened his belly, and cleaned him. I saved his liver, and was plenty careful how I dissected off the gall bladder. Then I skinned him and took off the meat. The best of it was along the back and down the tail, but I carved the legs too, so as not to miss anything. The meat and liver I stowed in a little bowl. The guts I threw out. The bones I put back in the pot and fed up the fire again, so it began to* simmer. *"You better make yourself comfortable. It's a long time before dinner."*

I aimed to boil about half that water away. It began to get dark and we lit the candles and watched and smelled. I washed off three eggs and dropped them in. When they were hard I fished them out, peeled them, and laid them in a bowl with the meat. She pounded up some coffee. After a long time that soup was almost done. Then something popped into my mind. "Listen, we got any paprika?"

"No, no paprika."

"Gee, we ought to have paprika."

"Pepper, salt, yes. No paprika."

"Go out there to the car and have a look. This stuff needs paprika, and it would be a shame not to have it just because we didn't look."

"I go, but is no paprika."

She took a candle and went back to the car. I didn't need any paprika. But I wanted to get rid of her so I could pull off something without any more talk about the sacrilegio. I took a candle and a machete and went back of the altar. There were four or five closets back there, and a couple of them were locked. I slipped the machete blade into one and snapped the lock. It was full of firecrackers for high mass and stuff for the Christmas crèche. I broke into another one. There it was, what I was looking for, six or eight bottles of sacramental wine. I grabbed a bottle, closed the closets, and came back. I dug the cork out with my knife and tasted it. It was A-1 sherry. I socked about a pint in the pot and hid the bottle. As soon as it heated up a little I lifted the pot off, dropped the meat in, sliced up the eggs, and put them in. I sprinkled in some salt and a little pepper.

She came back. "Is no paprika."

"It's all right. We don't need it. Dinner's ready."

We dug in.

Well, brother, you can have your Terrapin Maryland. It's a noble dish, but it's not Iguana John Howard Sharp. The meat is a little like chicken, a little like frog-legs, and a little like muskrat, but it's tenderer than any of them. The soup is one of the great soups of the world, and I've eaten Marseilles bouillabaisse, New Orleans crayfish bisque, clear green turtle, thick green turtle, and all kinds of other turtle there are. I think it was still better that we had to drink it out of bowls, and fish the meat out with a knife. It's gelatinous, and flooding up over your lips, it makes them sticky, so you can feel it as well as taste it.

*She drank hers stretched out on her belly, and after a while it occurred to me that if I got down and stuck my mouth up against hers, we would be stuck, so we experimented on that for a while. Then we drank some more soup, ate some more meat, and made the coffee. While we were drinking that she started to laugh. "Yeh? And what's so funny?"*
*"I feel—how you say? Dronk?"*
*"Probably born that way."*
*"I think you find wine. I think you steal wine, put in iguana."*
*"Well?"*
*"I like, very much."*
*"Why didn't you say so sooner?"*
*So I got out the bottle, and we began to swig it out of the neck. Pretty soon we were smearing her nipples with soup, to see if they would stick. Then after a while we just lay there, and laughed.*
*"You like the dinner?"*
*"It was lovely dinner,* gracias.*"*
*"You like the cook?"*
*"Yes . . . Yes . . . Yes. Very fonny cook."*

from *Serenade*

## Iguana John Howard Sharp

Boil meat of an iguana and set aside in a small bowl. Then fill a pot ⅔ full with water, add the bones of the iguana and bring to a boil. Boil three eggs and peel them. Add a pint of A-1 sherry to the boiling water, then drop the iguana meat in the pot. Slice the three eggs, put them in the boiling water and sprinkle in some salt and a little pepper.

When the water is boiled half away, the iguana soup is ready—and according to Cain, it tastes best served in church and on the nipples of a Mexican whore. The sherry, of course, should be sacramental wine. This was a pretty hot dish in 1937 and prompted Massachusetts to try, unsuccessfully, to ban *Serenade,* not only in Boston, but everywhere in the state.

# Black Bean Soup

Once, in a rather well-known San Francisco restaurant, Cain had the house's specialty—"Guatemala Black Bean Soup." Shortly thereafter, he was in Guatemala researching *Serenade* and he stopped by the Grand Hotel to check on the fine points of the soup, which he assumed they must serve. "I called the captain of the dining room, explained what I wanted, asked if I could talk with the chef and he retired to discuss the thing with the Maitre. They seemed perplexed and presently both of them came and assured me they'd never heard of it."

Cain persisted in his search and was not put off when someone in San Francisco told him the soup consisted of 1 can of Heinz black bean soup with lemon added. Where he finally found the recipe is not known, but this complex formula was found in his papers:

2 cups dried black beans

½ pound ham, cubed

3 quarts water

2 tablespoons olive oil

2 cloves garlic, minced

2 onions, chopped

1 carrot, sliced

½ cup chopped celery

1 green pepper, chopped

2 tomatoes, peeled and chopped

2 teaspoons salt

1 bay leaf

½ teaspoon dried ground chili peppers

1 teaspoon Spanish paprika

2 tablespoons butter

2 tablespoons flour

3 tablespoons run

6 thin slices lemon

3 hard-cooked egges, sliced

Wash the beans well and soak overnight in water to cover. Drain and rinse. Combine in a saucepan with the ham and 3 quarts water, bring to a boil, cover and cook over low heat 3 hours. Heat the oil in a skillet and sauté the garlic, onions, carrot, celery and green pepper 15 minutes. Add to the beans with the tomatoes, salt, bay leaf, chili peppers and paprika. Cover and cook over low heat 1 hour. Force the mixture through a sieve. Return to pan. Knead the butter and flour together and form into small balls. Add to soup, stirring to the boiling point. Taste for seasoning. Add the rum. Serve garnished with lemon and egg slices. Serves 6-8.

# Seven Years of Stew

Having had stew for supper every night for seven years and having discovered that he was to have stew yet another time, Alexander Libman leaped at his wife with a wild yell and began beating her. Without a doubt he did wrong. Respect for law is a basic principle in human society, and he should have called a policemen or something of the sort. But at the moment the legal phase of the case pales before the circumstances leading up to the battery: seven years of stew. Try to imagine seven years of stew! Seven times 365 is 2,555 and 2,555 suppers made of stew were served to Alexander Libman before he broke the law. The thing sets one's head reeling. After 2,555 suppers made of stew one would be dreaming of whole herds of stewing-beeves chasing about in meadows of onions, potatoes, celery and red peppers. It is enough to upset the whole Freud-Jung psychology.

*New York World* editorial
April 4, 1925

# FISH, GAME, & OTHER CAIN DISHES

□□□□□□□□□□□□□□□□□□□□□□□□□

## Shad Roe James M. Cain

When one cookbook compiler wrote asking for his "favorite dish," Cain responded with this recipe:

1 cup onions, chopped fine
1 cup cream
1 egg white
1 cup sherry
1 shad roe (2 pieces, the whole roe)

Fry onions in butter to golden brown, drain off butter. Beat up cream until it fluffs. Pull strings off shad roe, cut it up with egg beater, pull off remaining strings, if any, then beat well. Add egg white, beaten to froth and mix with beater. Add beaten cream, add onions, add sherry, salt and pepper. Turn into small baking dish, set in pan of water, and brown in hot oven (from 20 minutes to ½ hour).

# The Noble Catfish

One time, in connection with something I was writing, Massa Laurence Stallings and Colonel Morris Markey explained to me about catfish sandwiches. It seemed that these are very popular with the colored populations of Richmond, Va.; Atlanta, Ga., and other points South, and these two wights, when they really got warmed up, painted a picture of this outlandish delicacy that was fabulous in its rich, barbaric colors, much like the first act of *"Porgy."* It had me breathless, and then my eye caught an odd sort of manifestation in the vicinity of Stallings' mouth. This gifted lad was pouring out a veritable torrent of words on the Negro's strange love for catfish and all the time his own mouth was watering so copiously that a streamlet was drooling out of one corner of it.

It made an impression on me, for this Stallings, to say nothing of the colored race, knows a thing or two about good things to eat, and I thought of it the other night when I was in a fish market and saw a pile of nice, pink, skinned catfish. I bought a pound, five fish in all, had them wrapped up, and took them home. There I encountered a certain disdain, as it seemed catfish weren't elegant enough for them. It didn't feaze me. I gave directions how they were to be cooked: crumbed with a fine crumb and fried in butter, for at least I knew that much about them. When they were ready I sat down and ate them, all five of them, a whole pound of catfish.

Well, now, it is something to reach your dotage and then have a discovery like that waiting for you. This is one of the most distinguished fish that was ever taken on a hook. The meat has that quality which the Pacific sanddab has and which English sole has even more: a slight gumminess, so that it holds together instead of flaking apart, and you can really eat it instead of just picking at it. More importantly, it has taste. It is a rich, dark taste, quite different from any fish taste I have ever had; such a taste as sent me down the next night for two pounds, as they didn't seem to be quite as snooty at home after they saw me put down the first batch.

Now, I suppose catfish isn't exactly news any more and I ought not to be taking up about one-half ton of white paper telling how I first tasted it. But I know what I am doing. In all the thousands of times I have eaten in restaurants I don't recall once having seen "Fried

Catfish" on the menu, and so I have become a man with a mission. I am going to make this country catfish conscious. I am going to find a wine that goes with it and plug that. I am going into the question of a new name for it, for, obviously, its name is what ails it. Ordinarily, I dislike making liberty cabbage out of sauerkraut, but if a new name is what the catfish needs to get into polite society, a new name it shall have. I am going to put this fish over. When I get through Stallings will have to hang a siphon on his mouth to receive company at all.

Hearst Column
December 27, 1933

# Renaming the Catfish

I have been going into this question of another name for the catfish (as indicated yesterday), in order that it may take its place on elegant menus, and win the acclaim to which its quality entitles it. So doing, I have borne in mind the fight made by the avocado growers, who have recently got rid of the word "alligator pear," which had plagued them for years. Their point was that not only was "alligator pear" an ugly term, with associations distasteful to the delicate imagination, and not only was it a gross libel, since the fruit was neither a pear nor was it eaten by alligators, but that it was a downright misnomer, since the proper designation, from the time the Spaniards landed in Central America, is "avocado." So, primed with valid arguments, they won their battle, and the person who persists in "alligator pear" nowadays seems a little behind the times.

It behooved me, then, to find out what the catfish was called before rough mouths tasted it, and rough tongues found a name for it. That meant an Indian word, and after considerable thumbing through the dictionaries I found three, as follows:

Biloxi Language: Cka.

Choctaw Language: Nakishwana.

Osage Language: Tuce.

Of these the first makes no impression on me whatever, and besides I haven't the faintest notion how to pronounce it. The second, undeniably, has a great deal to be said for it. It is one of those fish names, like pompano, bonita and barracuda, that is highly colorful, but on just that score, I am afraid, it will have to be rejected. The trouble with these names is that they are too colorful: they don't suggest fish on the table, but fish on the hook, with a gallant angler bringing them up to the gaff; they prick your imagination, but they don't make you hungry.

This leaves the third, and I think it is what we have been looking for. All good fish names, so far as the diners are concerned, are of one syllable, like trout, bass, perch, rock, cod, shad, and sole. Tuce would be a plausible addition to this list, and sound like a fish meant to be eaten, not photographed. I therefore call on all patriotic restaurateurs to give the catfish a tryout under this name, and see what happens. I anticipate a hit.

The question of a suitable wine I haven't got around to yet. Pending a report on that, you can stick to Pouilly. When it is a question of fish, you can't go very wrong on that.

Hearst column
December 30, 1933

# But What Matters Less Than The Catfish?

Some time ago, you may recall, I renamed the catfish. I felt its monicker was against it, and looked up another for it in an Indian dictionary; I decreed that henceforth it should be known as tuce, and in hog signo conquer the world.

And thereby hangs a tale. Moneta, in New York, accepted my dictum, and called the fish tuce. He didn't only do that. Once he had called it tuce, and studied out an enticing way to fix it, he named the dish after me. Believe it or not, he named it Tuce Fish Alla Cain, and so entered it on his menu card. Well, you know how that is. If a Third Avenue coffee pot had named a dish after me, that would have been agreeable, but not exciting. But when Moneta names a dish after me, that is an event in my life, for Moneta's is one of the restaurants of the world, a place to go to when all is dark and drear, and damply drops the tear: it *never* lets you down.

So, being in New York over a weekend, I went down there of a Saturday night, to call on Moneta, and thank him for the honor, and if possible, taste the dish. He didn't have it that night, but he was enormously pleased with it, as it had turned out highly profitably, as I had predicted, in this very space, it would be.

"It's a foney t'ing," said Moneta. "I try dees fish, maybe ten year ago. I try'm once, twice, maybe t'ree time. Nobody eat dees fish at all. Was, how you say? Was a flop. Was one hell of a flop. Then now, I call'm Tuce Fish Alla Cain, fish go fine. Ever'body likes dees fish. Call'm catfish, nobody eat'm at all. Call'm Tuce Fish, sell plenty. Is fine."

So then, of course, we made a date. We made a date to eat the fish. I was to come in there Monday, at noon sharp, and then, with a bottle of suitable wine, we would sit down and try this enchanting dish. But, alas, it laid an egg. The Fulton Fish Market, on Monday, has disappointed many an eager lad before Moneta, and when I got there on Monday he didn't have the fish. When he found out it was imperative that I leave New York that afternoon, he began to mope. I am informed he moped a week and was even observed on one occasion wiping his eyes and blowing his nose.

Well, ain't that tough on the old boy. Do you know what this is going to cost *me*? It's going to cost me one round trip ticket on the choo choo cars, $167. It's going to cost me Pullman charges both ways, $50. It is going to cost me meals, tips, hotel bills, taxi fares, $300, more or less. It's going to cost me ten days of my time, going and coming. All that it's going to cost me to eat that fish, and keep Moneta's heart from being broken, and to claim a great moral victory in the matter of a new monicker for the catfish.

And all for what? Can you tell me of anything of less public importance, in this hour of national crisis, than what the catfish is called? Can you tell me of anything that matters less than a catfish?

Hearst column
June 25, 1934

# Tuce Fish à la Cain

Take 1 pound of skinned catfish, crumb with a fine crumb and fry in butter.

# The Muskrat or Aquaba Maryland à la Cain

Some time ago, in this place, I did a great service to the catfish by giving it another name. After conning a few Indian dictionaries I decreed it should be called *Tuce*; using this monniker, restaurant men put it on their menus, and it was a hit. Perhaps the fact that they named the dish after me had something to do with it; I shouldn't be surprised. Well, I now proceed to do a similar service to another delicacy that has suffered from its name; to wit, the muskrat.

This animal, while scientifically classified as a rat, deserves none of the odium that its wharf cousins have brought upon it. That is, it is in no sense a scavenger, being on the contrary a most fastidious animal in the matter of the food that it eats. It lives chiefly on the roots of marsh lilies and reeds, which it washes clean before it even considers taking a bite. In addition, it consumes occasional mussels. Its general habits are impeccable. It lives in houses made of grass and mud, which it builds with its tail. The entrances are under water, so it always goes to bed well washed. In other words, it has the soul of a beaver, which is just what this country needs today.

The meat is dark, about the color of duck. It is tender, and of a fine, rich flavor, much better than squirrel or rabbit. It can be fried and served with brown gravy, but in my opinion it is best when served as mock terrapin. The process is the same as for Terrapin Maryland, except that you use muskrat instead of terrapin. I'm not kidding you: this is a dish.

For a name, I have looked in several Indian dictionaries, and find these: Navajo language, *Tqaba Mai;* Chinook language, *Eminepu;* Biloxi language, *Xanaxka.* Personally, I think all of these leave something to be desired, so I have made a sort of free combination of the Navajo word and the Biloxi word, getting *Aquaba.* This vaguely suggests an animal that lives in the water, and I think it is a winner.

A word now to the restaurant trade: Muskrats are cheap, as the carcasses go begging after the fur is sold. You can make a handsome dish out of this, with a nice profit, if you go about it right and handle it with some confidence. Use a tureen and serve on toast. Price it at least $1.35. And, of course, name it Aquaba Maryland à la Cain. That puts the lucky spot on it.

Hearst column
January 7, 1935

# Them Ducks

The first thing you must get through your head, if you are plotting a wild duck dinner, is that there is something silly about the whole rite. You simply cannot get away with it if you do it as you would do an ordinary dinner, with your wife at one end of the table, yourself at the other, and rows of politely dressed ladies and gentlemen in between. You try that, and you are in for a flop. The reason is that some of these people will show their manners by ignoring your hocus-pocus, others will show their sense of humor by giggling at it, and all of them will show a lamentable ignorance as to what it is all about. Bow your head, then, to reality. Banish dressing. Banish politeness. Banish women. In other words, keep your eye on this central principle: when it comes to something faintly absurd, as this is, the male gender has a much greater capacity for punishment than the female, a much greater inclination to accept it with becoming solemnity—so that you should make the thing stag.

Moreover, when you pick your stags, pick those who are epicures, or think they are. It may seem risky, if this is your first try at it, to submit your efforts to the judgment of such critics, but really it is not. You see, when you take them out and look at them, there ain't no such animiles as epicures. They are their own optical illusion. They have no such knowledge as they imagine they have, for no such knowledge exists. You are perfectly safe with them, then, for they will be owlishly patient if something goes sour, will nod sagely and mutter encouragingly even if you have to do it all over again, and thus confer an agreeable air of importance on the show. And when it is all over, they will give you applause more satisfactory than you could get from anybody else. For when you come right down to it, there are only two ways in which they can exhibit their imaginary diplomas; one, by saying everything is lousy; two, by saying everything is great. Well, saying everything is lousy doesn't get them anywhere. It is a theme, somehow, that doesn't orchestrate; it brings the curtain down with a bang, and then they have to talk about something else. But saying everything is great—there's a theme. It goes places, invites comparisons, permits them to set the way you do it beside the way it was done at a little restaurant in Copenhagen, and of course Copenhagen leads to Paris, and Paris to Warsaw, and Warsaw to Hong Kong, with its incomparable shark-fin soup. It's all talk but when the cigars finally come you will have a warm, expansive feeling, will think of yourself as a chevalier-at-large in a wide, wide world, will be established as a *bonvivant* who knows how to cut up ducks, and really knows.

So much, then, for the general approach: we shall now take up the thing itself. I warn you that it is appallingly expensive, at least in initial outlay, although once that has been made, game ducks don't cost much more than any other kind of ducks. First, then, you will have to go to a restaurant supply house and get yourself a duck press. This will cost you about $20, and you will have to have it. Ducks without a duck press are like turkey without cranberry sauce; possible, but hardly conceivable. You will have to get a chafing dish, if you haven't one already, and this will set you back something too. Be sure to get one with a controllable flame. And, of course, you will have to get the ducks. If you have friends who shoot, they will often give you some, just to make you feel like a poor relative; if not, a few discreet inquiries, at your favorite restaurant for instance, will usually put you on the track of some. They have laws about ducks, you see, and sometimes a little money has to pass, but if you mean it, you can get them. Out West, they raise Mallards from eggs, and no laws are involved in these at all. It is heretical to say so, but I don't see much difference between Mallards raised in a coop and Mallards shot on a creek. If they are properly fed, they have an excellent flavor, and there is this to be said for them: you can get them when you want them.

When you have connected with the ducks, make up your party. I suggest that you under-invite, rather than over-invite. Three ducks, theoretically, will serve six persons, but I would only invite three besides yourself. The extra duck will do for second helpings, and there will be an impression of plenty that a duck dinner all-too-frequently lacks. Now then, arrange for the rest of your dinner. For soup, I would serve clear green turtle. It smacks of salt water and yet isn't outright fishy. Have good big plates of it, and hop it up well with sherry; a duck dinner should be very winey from the outset. There is one danger with this soup: the cook, when she puts the wine in, commonly neglects to give it time to heat before serving, so that it often comes in cold. See that it comes in hot. You don't make it, by the way, by buying a 150-pound turtle and boiling it. It comes in cans, at fancy groceries, and in any of the standard brands it's as good as it ever gets.

After the soup, shoot the duck. That's what they came for, and you shouldn't delay it with a fish course, or a lobster course, or any other course you may have heard of just to be fancy. Furthermore, it is essential that they be reasonably hungry by the time the duck comes on. For one vegetable, fried hominy is obligatory. For another, wild rice is not obligatory, but expected. For another, sweet potatoes do very well, but don't have them candied, as this will muck up a plate already pretty well-smeared with sauce. Currant jelly is also put on the table. A salad is a good idea, but it should be simply romaine, lettuce, endive, or cress with a French dressing. For dessert, you can't do better than an ice, and the tarter and simpler the better, as a quick change from the heavy eating that has gone before. For wine, you can get by with a dry sherry, but I don't recommend it. The whole dinner is a little on the sherry side, and I think a red Burgundy is much better. Be sure it is imported: there is no sense in going to all this trouble, and then louse your show up with a domestic wine that may turn out quite different from what you expected. All our American wines are very spotty, and this is no time for idle experiment. Champagne, as they are just finishing the duck, is permissible, but again I don't recommend it. It is a little amateurish, too much of a good thing: your gang will be a little relieved if they don't have to tackle it. Get still Burgundy. That dreadful stuff known as sparkling Burgundy will make the whole thing a flop.

Now, then, for the ducks. The whole trick, here, is in timing, and as the maid figures in it just as importantly as you do, you will have to coach her patiently, so that she knows every move she has to make. This is the way the thing goes:

1. Maid comes in with paraphernalia for sauce, as soon as she has poured wine and removed soup plates, and places it on the table, to your left.

2. Ducks, on word from you, go into oven.

3. You make the sauce, at the table, all except for blood, which goes in last.

4. Ducks come in, and you carve them.

5. Carcasses go into press, blood is pressed out, add to sauce.

6. Carved portions go into sauce, are put on plates, and passed.

The maid, obviously, is the key to all this. She comes in, with the soup plates out of the way, with the following stuff: the chafing dish, a cruet with sherry in it, a small plate with pieces of butter on it and a half lemon; a saucer with one or two spoonfuls of currant jelly on it; a bottle of Worcestershire sauce, salt, pepper and paprika. Have her bring these on a tray, and take them off *yourself,* and place them on the table, to your left. If you put them at your right, you are going to foul your carving arm badly. You take them off yourself, in order to inventory them, and make sure they are all there, and make sure, too, that you know where they are when you reach for them. Once this thing starts, you are out of luck if you have to stop while she trots back to the kitchen for something she has forgotten. If she has forgotten something, send her back for it now.

When this stuff has all been checked and is on the table, take out your watch, say "Time!" and lay it on the table. Brother, I caution you above all else to do this, and not rely on any promises made by the cook to do these ducks so they will knock your eye out. There is no cook in the world, except the chefs in the very best restaurants, who really believes that nine minutes are enough for ducks. I said *nine,* not one second more, not one second less, count 'em: one, two, three, four, five, six, seven, eight, nine. If you don't hold your own watch on them, they will be cooked twelve, fifteen or even twenty minutes, and then you are sunk. If they are cooked that long, they won't have any taste, and worse yet they won't have any blood; all your press, sauce and everything else will look completely ridiculous, and you will wish to God you had never started this thing at all. Once again, just so you won't forget it: nine minutes. Those ducks, after having a handful of ordinary celery wadded into them, go into an oven as hot as the cook can make it, and at the end of nine minutes, they come out of that oven and come straight on the table.

All right, then, we are back again, now, at the table: the maid has gone to tell the cook to put the ducks in. When she comes back, she brings the press with her and places it on a small table beside you, at your left, and stands by, like a nurse at an operation, without leaving you for a second, except on her cue, as we shall see.

What you do, as soon as you have called "Time!" is start on the first part of the sauce. You light the chafing dish. You put in several pieces of butter, let them melt. You pour in sherry. As to how much butter, and how much sherry, you will use a little judgment, depending on how many there are at table. There should be about half melted butter and half sherry. Don't let this boil, and don't stir it. Take the chafing dish, lift it from the flame a little, and gently shake it to blend the butter and the wine together. Add a teaspoonful of the currant jelly, keep shaking until it dissolves evenly. Squirt in a few drops of lemon. Add one teaspoonful of Worcestershire sauce. Salt a little, pepper a little, paprika a little. Keep shaking until you have a nice even mixture, set the dish down again, cut the flame low and let it alone. Don't be alarmed that it seems dreadfully thin, and has a sickly color. All that will change later. If you don't take my word for it, take the word of Moneta in New York, Marconi in Baltimore, Perino in Los Angeles, and other celebrated maestri of this dish. It'll be all right, if you don't force it, and you don't worry about it.

Now then, look at your watch and keep looking at it. Don't worry about conversation at this point. If you have invited the right mob, it will be quiet, restrained, and interested: you will have no sense of dragging time, no worry about whether your party is a flop. These boys will carry you through: they know what you are feeling. When nine minutes have gone by, shoot the maid out into the kitchen as fast as she can go and make her get those ducks. As we have seen, the cook will be hostile to the idea of taking them out, but make her get them. She brings them in on a very hot platter, and then you do some more of your stuff. The platter goes right in front of you, and you carve the ducks at once. You carve them with a smallish fork and a smallish, thin moderately curved knife. It should be a knife of sufficient body, however, that you can throw your strength into it if you have to, and you may have to.

Now all your life you have heard a lot of talk about how these ducks are carved, and most of it is hooey. You do, it is true, take off the whole breast, wing and leg in one piece, and serve that piece as a portion. You do, it is true, do it with "one cut of the knife," and you are supposed to do it with a fair show of speed. But this traditional description of the business somehow evokes a wrong picture, and you had better get the right picture, for if you don't, you are going to try to do something that is downright impossible, like rolling a cigarette with one hand. In the first place, it is a ticklish job, and you mustn't try to hurry it. It won't take long, no matter how you do it. In the second place, that "one cut of the knife" business is somewhat misleading. You do make "one cut of the knife," but it is a careful, painstaking cut, in which the knife is worked down with little short, sawing motions, and in which, when a joint if struck, you press outward, with the heel of the blade, to give yourself all the help from leverage that you can. Put the fork in, then, on the left side of the breast, when the neck is away from you, and start your cut, on the right side of the breast, as near the breast bone as you can. Work down rapidly, against the bone, until you come to the wing. This will come off with no trouble at all. Cut quickly down to the leg, and say a prayer. If you hit the joint squarely, it should come off too, and you can cut the whole portion clear in a jiffy. But it *may* not come clean and you had better not trifle with it. Don't be too proud, on this occasion, to have a joint cutter in your boot. This is a small contrivance that looks like a pair of pruning shears, and you could cut a thumb off with it if you had to. Get it in there, and get it in quick: cut the joint, get the portion off, reverse your duck and do the same for the other side, and get on to the next ducks. Pack the portions close together on the platter, for warmth. If the platter is as hot as it should be, they will keep hot long enough.

All right now, you are pretty near home. The maid, all this time, is at your elbow. You take those carcasses with the fork, and you clap them into the duck press. Under the spout, the maid has placed a saucer. She now turns the press while you hold its legs, and the blood begins to run. When you have most of it, pick up the saucer and have her take the press away, and come back with the hot plates. Add the blood to the sauce a very little at a time, shaking the chafing dish gently as before. If you don't get panicky and dump the blood in all at once, so that it curdles into the worst mess you ever saw in your life, the sauce will steadily thicken and gain color and smell. When the saucer of blood is all in, spoon in the few puddles of blood that remain on the platter. Your sauce is now ready. Leave the flame burning low, and dip each portion of duck smartly into the sauce, so that it is well soaked. Serve on the hot plates. Have the maid get busy with the hominy, the rice and the sweet potatoes. That is your wild duck dinner.

When they are a little bit along, give the word for the extra duck, or ducks, to go into the oven. Have the maid hold the watch and bring them in at the proper time. These ducks you can slice, as you would turkey. Don't bother with a second making of sauce. There will be enough in there to wet a few pieces more.

Pat yourself on the back. Quaff your Burgundy. Accept your plaudits. Reflect that you are probably a crack-brained fool, but then who isn't?

*Esquire,* January 1935

# Recipe: Wild Duck

Stuff duck with handful of ordinary celery, bake in hot oven for only 9 minutes and do not let the cook or anyone else convince you otherwise. "There is no cook in the world, except the chefs in the very best restaurants, who believe that 9 minutes are enough for ducks." Also, buy six ducks, which theoretically will feed six people, but invite only three other epicureans, then there will be an impression of plenty that a duck dinner all-too-frequently lacks.

*Sauce:* Prepare in chafing dish, lit beside you on the table. Put in several pieces of butter, let them melt, then pour in sherry, about half butter and half sherry, total amount depending on the number of guests. Do not let it boil and do not stir; lift chafing dish from flame and gently shake to blend; add a tablespoonful of currant jelly and continue shaking until jelly dissolves. Squirt in a few drops of lemon and add one teaspoonful of Worcestershire sauce. Add a touch of salt, pepper and paprika. When the mixture is blended, set the dish down, lower the flame and let it alone. "Don't be alarmed that it seems dreadfully thin and has a sickly color. All that will change later. If you don't take my word for it, take the word of Moneta in New York, Marconi in Baltimore, Perino in Los Angeles and other celebrated maestri of this dish."

# How To Carve That Bird

Friends, if you want the cook to take the bows after that turkey dinner, list and learn somewhere else, for there is a mighty literature on how to get this bird ready for the table; but if you want to take the bows yourselves, you will do what I tell you, for carving turkey isn't as easy as it looks, and it doesn't look any too easy, at that.

The first consideration in getting a turkey apart, then, is speed. Step on it, brother. And if stepping on it compromises your impressive, leisurely dignity, step on it anyhow; for what your impressive, leisurely dignity will look like if you take too long about it, and the party at the other end of the table calls time on you, and comes rushing around to take charge of things herself, or worse yet, summons a pinch hitter to relieve you at the platter is something too dreadul for words to describe. You will have piled up a fiasco on yourself that will haunt you to the last day of your life.

It is advisable, in view of this, to pass up the $25 gift carving set you got for your last birthday. It will work, of course, but by the time you have figured out what all the gadgets are and have whetted the knife twenty times, to make it cut, and have straightened the fork where it twisted in its buckhorn handle, and have discovered that the steel is really a rat-tail file, it will be too late, and you will wish you hadn't. Go to the best hardware store in town, or still better, to the best restaurant supply house, and get yourself some tools that a chef would be proud to own. Never mind what they look like. Here again it is a question whether the jewelry store takes the bows, or you do. Get a knife of the best steel, one that balances nicely when *you* take hold of it. Don't get a knife too big: this is a turkey, not a whale. A blade nine inches long is about right; it should have some depth at the hilt, so you have plenty of knife; it should be only slightly curved, and should taper gracefully to the point, as this shape knife is best for slicing. Get a good big fork with curved prongs, one that will stay where you put it, and lift if you want it to, without slipping out and dropping a carcass in somebody's lap. Get a steel. Get an emery stone. Don't bring this to the table, but use it before the guests arrive, this way: using the fine side of the stone, lay the hilt of the knife across it at about a thirty-degree angle, the edge toward you. Draw the knife across the stone, *toward* you, lightly, without pressing on it. Reverse and do the same for the other side. About a dozen strokes sharpen it. The steel you will have to use at the table. Here again, whet *toward* the edge, not away from it. With the steel in your left hand, the knife in your right, put the point of the steel against the hilt of the knife. Draw the knife across the steel, reverse at once, do the same thing for the other side. Keep this up smartly, for about a dozen strokes, which will be enough. Perhaps you had better practice this in secret. If you make a mislick with everybody looking at you, and cut your thumb, it would be rather unfortunate.

We are still, remember, on the subject of speed. To that see that the maid doesn't wait until all the soup plates have been removed before she brings in the turkey. As soon as your plate is taken, have her bring it in. This will give you a precious two- or three-minute start. If you are right-handed, see that she sets it down with the tail and legs to your right: if you don't watch her, she will do it backwards, and you will have to right it, and will lose what you have gained. If you are left-handed, have the legs and tail to your left.

See that no garnishings of any kind whatever are served on the platter: with brown potatoes, or a pile of wild rice, not even Delmonico himself could manage the dish without making a mess of it.

You can now stand up, for I wouldn't attempt the bravura of carving while sitting down. The gag you stand up on is up to you, but the best gag is none at all. Let others do the gagging, for not all your wit can save you now, unless you deliver some turkey with it, and deliver pretty quickly at that. Hear what they say, but smilingly, not laughingly: a turkey is there looking at you, and it won't march off the plates by itself. So once more: step on it, brother, step and step again.

First, sink the fork at a spot an inch or two abaft the point of the breastbone, square across the middle, one prong on one side, the other prong on the other side. If you hit bone, come out at once, and try a point a little farther aft. The place is there, don't worry about that. And when you sink it in, sink it. Don't half do it, so the turkey is skating all over the platter, like a gun loose at sea.

Slip the point of the knife under the first wing and make an upward cut, as far as you can. And here again: when you cut, cut. Decision counts more than anatomical accuracy, for remember this is a cooked bird, not a live one, and its inclination is to come apart, rather than stay together. As soon as you have made this cut, make a downward cut, for the joint that holds the wing to the turkey, a straight cut well toward the neck, so as not to undershoot the joint. The wing should now drop off. If it doesn't, get the knife into the joint at once and get it off, by breaking if necessary. I caution you right now that the underdone turkey, with tough joints, and the overdone turkey, which falls apart, are both hazards that you must be ready for. What with the late cook and the late guest, there is hardly any such thing as a perfectly cooked turkey, and you had better be ready for grief, whatever way it comes.

When the wing drops, let it stay where it is, and don't do anything about it for the time being. It will come into the picture only when it is time for second helpings, and it only slows up the show to cut it up now. Step on it, brother, and keep stepping: you are out in the middle, they are all looking at you, their cruel gaping jaws want turkey and turkey is the only thing that will satisfy them, so you haven't time even to think about that wing. Cut off the leg, and do it at once. Make a straight cut for the joint that holds it to the turkey, first cutting away all strings. Cut an inch or two above the pope's nose, going as far as you can. Now slip the knife behind the leg, and cut for the joint again. The leg should now fall. If it doesn't, get the knife in the joint, turn it, and break the leg off. You have to get it off, and get it off quick. If you can't do it gracefully, get it off anyhow, even if it makes a loud crack: a laugh is better than a stage wait, and the show doesn't go on until that leg is off.

Once it is off, what you do with it will tell the whole story as to how well you are going to do this job. The next step is to get it in half, one half called the second joint, the other half the drumstick. Get the fork in the second joint, and cut for the joint that holds the drumstick, holding the knife so you can brace against the drumstick. As soon as you have cut, turn and push the knife outward so you break it. Break it, and break it quickly. As soon as it is broken, one or two cuts will sever it clean. Now then, cut up the second joint. Get the fork into it, and slice off as many pieces of the dark meat as you can. Do the same for the drumstick, catching the small end of it with the fork, and slicing off the meat as well as you can, but not stopping to do an absolutely clean job of it: there are always a few shreds of meat hanging to the bone.

Now then, let us stop a moment and have a look at the geography of your platter. Northeast is a wing, still lying there where you left it. Due east are two bones, and a pile of sliced dark meat. Due west is the main turkey. Very well, push the two bones up beside the wing. Push the dark meat up near it. This is to clear the eastern part of the platter for the breast, which you are now ready to carve.

Whet your knife. You have been cutting joints with it, and if you don't put it on the steel, you are not going to slice, you are going to mangle. Sink the fork into the two holes that mark where you had it in the first place. Tilt the turkey toward you, so you will be slicing in a horizontal plane. *Don't* try to slice vertically, so the slices will fall outward as they do in the ham advertisements. This is turkey, not ham, and while they will fall if you do it that way, they will also fall to pieces. Slice so that each slice lies in place until you lift it carefully down with the knife. Slice with an easy, light motion, but with a confident motion, too. Slice as thin as you can, and in a plane that yields you the largest slices possible. Be careful, when you lift each slice down, not to break it, and to pile it neatly in the place you have left for it. When you hit bone, get the last few slivers off with the point of the knife, and lift them down too.

Now serve the first plates, and if I were you, I wouldn't have them brought until right now. In the first operations, they will be in your way, and they will be getting cold. The maid should put them in front of you when you get the first side of the turkey carved, which is where you are at this time. Now let us have a second look at the geography of your platter. If you have done it as I told you to do it, you have, northeast, a wing, two bones, and a pile of dark meat. You have, east, a pile of white meat. And you have, south, the opening from which you will get your stuffing. Very well, then, cut the strings, dig in with the spoon, and give the first plate its stuffing. On top of that lay a slice of white meat. Beside that put a piece of second joint and a small piece of drumstick. Have the maid take it away, and do the same for the next plate. All your platter is in perfect order for the serving, and you still haven't taken an undue amount of time. Furthermore, when four of five plates have been served, you have come out even on that side of the turkey, and can start the second side without a messy pile fouling you on the other side of the platter. You needn't be alarmed at the person who sings out "Only white meat for me, please." As a matter of fact, there is more white meat than dark on a turkey, and getting rid of an extra slice of it will simplify things, not aggravate them.

For the second half of the turkey, proceed as you did with the first half, except that there is a sloppiness permissible here that you couldn't have got away with on the first half. That is, you don't carve everything up complete, but only to the extent that is necessary to complete the serving. If you are ambidextrous, and can use the knife as well with your left hand as you can with your right, you will have no trouble; if you are hopelessly unidextral, you may have to put the fork in near the wing joint, and slice the breast toward the breastbone instead of away from it. I suggest to you that unless you have an enormous mob to feed, it is well to get a turkey big enough to yield the complete first serving from one side, and then the thing becomes much simpler. But whatever you do, do it quick, and always remember that very important thing: keep the geography of your platter clearly in mind, so you can do your stuff without getting hopelessly snowed under with wings, legs, white meat, dark meat, bones, stuffing, and string.

It's no cinch, but if you insist on doing it, that is the way it will work, and no other way. Oh, and one more thing. For heaven's sake, don't try Moselles, strange and improbable Bordeaux, and other such wines with this fowl. They won't drink them, I'm telling you, they won't drink them. You just won't make a sale. Good old Chablis is the stuff to serve; it's a little shy on originality, but it goes down their throats. Well, God bless you and don't say I didn't warn you.

*Esquire,* December 1934

# Recipe: Steamed Turkey with Oysters and Dumplings Bechamel-Mencken

This concoction was the creation of Henry Mencken, who professed to find it wonderful. So Cain and his fourth wife, Florence, fixed it so they could "serve the dish to him with a grin our face," Cain said, "in case he ever came out there." But Mencken never got out to California or over to Cain's house in Hyattsville, after they moved East, to sample the dish.

*To prepare the turkey:*

Pat a 10-12 lb. turkey dry and rub all over (and inside cavity) with salt and pepper. Stuff the cavity with:

2 large onions, split and stuck with 4 cloves

2 stalks celery, with green tops
4-6 sprigs parsley
2-3 sprigs thyme
12-15 peppercorns
1 large carrot, grated
In a steamer or roaster, prepare stock of:
4 qts. water
the turkey neck, giblets (except liver)
3 cloves garlic
1 onion, quartered
1 carrot
2 sprigs parsley
1 stalk celery
2 bay leaves
2 sprigs thyme
Simmer 25 min. and set turkey on rack above the stock.
Cover roaster tightly and cook 20 min. per pound until
juices run clear when upper part of turkey leg is stuck with
a fork. Remove turkey to a platter and keep warm. Reserve
stock.
*To prepare the oysters:*
Put in stainless steel or enamel pot
3 pts. oysters (standards)
1 tbsp butter
1 tbsp worcestershire
½ tsp nutmeg
salt, pepper and Tobasco to taste
Heat gently until juices bubble and edges of oysters curl
(oysters are scalded). Drain oysters, reserving juice.
*To make bechamel sauce:*
Measure oyster liquer and add turkey stock to equal 3
cups.
In saucepan, melt 3 tbsp butter and stir-blend, to make
a roux, 3 tbsp flour. Cook, stirring 3 mins., then stir in,
in a stream, as much of the 3 cups liquer-stock as needed
for a fairly thick sauce. Stirring, bring gradually to boil.
Simmer 5 min., to desired thickness. Set aside to keep
warm. (When the oysters are put with the stock, they'll
thin it a bit more.)

*To prepare dumplings:*

Drain juices from turkey into the stock, adjust seasoning and allow to continue simmering while the dough is prepared:

Sift together into a large bowl

   3 cups all-purpose flour

   1½ tbsp. baking powder

   ½ tbsp salt

Stir in 3 eggs mixed with 1 c. milk and 1 c. parsley leaves, snipped

It should be a fairly stiff dough.

Drop by rounded tbsp into the stock, keeping the dumplings separated.

Cover the pot tightly, keep the stock simmering, and cook 15 min. until light and cooked through (adapted from James Beard's directions).

Scoop dumplings out of stock and combine in a buttered baking dish with the oysters.

Pour bechamel over all and, if desired, top with

   ½ c. parmesan, grated and mixed with

   1 c/ soft bread crumbs

Put under broiler 5 min., serve immediately with the turkey.

# Spaghetti

Spaghetti, like steak, eggs, and hot dogs, is one of the irreducible simplicities of eating, and it is precisely these simplicities which must be right to the last decimal point of each person's taste, or they can hardly be eaten at all. One can accept Sole Marguery in the style of the chef that cooks it, but let a steak come medium when one ordered rare, one can hardly eat it at all and the dinner is ruined.

It is important to remember, then, that spaghetti begets individual preference, and that any effort to knock your guests cold with Spaghetti Caruso, Spaghetti Neapolitan, or spaghetti in any style that makes a set, formal dish out of it, is almost sure to flop. The spaghetti supper should be organized so each guest can have it as he likes it, with meat sauce or with tomato sauce, or with meat sauce and tomato sauce mixed, or with tomato sauce worked through the strands and the meat sauce nested on top, or *al dente,* or medium, or well done, or in any of the idiotic combinations that people get addicted to, and have to have, or be unhappy.

Nevertheless, certain principles govern the dish, and these should be observed if success is to be achieved. It should be borne in mind, for example, that spaghetti is no dish to invite people to, or to serve as part of a regular dinner, or to make plans about at all. The reason is that it requires such intimacy between table and stove that it cannot be managed in an elegant way without being unfit to eat. It is essentially an informal, pick-up affair, something to hit upon around eleven at night, when the party is sagging a bit and the guests look hungry. The corollary of this principle is that any notion you may have of making the sauces in your own kitchen is all wrong. No party can wait that long, and if you do it in advance, that element gets into it that which I have just spoken of: elaborate preparation, which is fatal. Also, the sauces are about five times as much trouble as you think, and while you may make them once you won't make them twice, and spaghetti ceases to be a regular part of your life. If you insist, I append a couple of recipes that tell how the thing is done, but I warn you you'll wish you hadn't.

The way to manage the sauce question is to find a restaurant that makes sauces to your taste, and then drop by once a week, taking home what you need in jars, and then you have it in the ice box when you want it. I get mine from Perino, in Los Angeles, who furnished me with the recipes below, and for me it works out fine. Don't get the idea, by the way, that spaghetti is a particularly cheap dish, as many seem to think. Good spaghetti sauce costs something, whether Perino makes it or you make it. But on the other hand, it isn't outlandishly expensive, and it is worth something to get it right.

The next principle to be noted is that to get spaghetti, you must go where spaghetti is. You cannot get spaghetti, or anything that goes with it, in an American grocery, regardless of what they tell you about the fine quality of the goods they carry. There is no package spaghetti, or package cheese, that is fit to eat, and that is all the American stores carry. To get spaghetti you have to go to Italians: nobody else understands it. Within a mile of you, if you take the trouble to find it, is an Italian grocery, and that is where you go to get your material. What you chiefly need is the spaghetti itself, arranged in wooden bins, about a hundred different sizes of spaghetti, ranging from fine sizes for soups, sometimes sold as Capelli d'angelo, or "Angel's Hair," to coarse macaronis. For myself, I use a medium small size, but you will have to find one to suit you. I suggest, if spaghetti is a new idea to you, that you take home a small quantity of several different sizes, cook them up, and see which you like best. But once you have settled on it, stock your spaghetti several pounds at a time, as it is a nuisance to be going after it constantly. Most Italians know enough not to break spaghetti, but if a stupid clerk tries to do it, stop him. Spaghetti is only good when the bunch is put in the pot whole. In an Italian grocery, ready-grated cheese is unknown. They will cut off a hunk of Fromaggio Romano and grate it while you wait, packing it in a little carton. In that way it is fresh when you need it, with a beautiful aroma peculiar to itself.

The next principle to be noted is that there is only one way to get spaghetti on the plate without having it stick together in a glutinous mass, unfit to eat and horrible even to look at. On this subject there is more misinformation going around than you can even keep track of, and I warn you against all of it. You will be told to put the spaghetti through a sieve, to get rid of the water, and then serve it. Wrong: it will stick. You will be told that if it gets sticky in the sieve, to run a little cold water over it, and that will loosen it up. Wrong: it will still stick, and be cold in addition. You will be told that if is sticks in the sieve, a little warm butter poured over it will loosen it up. Wrong: it will stick, and be full of butter as well. You will be told to cook the spaghetti in advance, drain it, and put it away in the ice box for heating when needed, and then it won't stick. Wrong: it will stick, and taste warmed-up as well. You will be told to hold the lid over the pot, drain the water off the spaghetti, then turn it out in a chafing dish, where it will keep hot while being served. Wrong: it will coagulate into a mass like old paper-hanger's paste, and be totally unfit to eat.

This is the one way that will work: Dig down into the pot with a big fork, hook up a wad, experience will have to teach you how much, and lift it high above your head, until every strand is clear of the pot. Hold it there a moment, until the water has dripped off, then swing it over the plate of the guest that is to eat it. Then down with it. That is all. Pot to plate is the way to serve spaghetti, with no sieve, chafing dish, ice box, or anything else intervening. This way, and this way alone, you can serve spaghetti hot, unstuck, and edible. This is the most important principle of all, and I beg you to bear it in mind, and not be led stray by the pet schemes which people will try to sell you. With these main points stated, we now come to the way to proceed. Once spaghetti is voted the order of the night, go out into the kitchen, get out a big stewpan, half fill it with water, put in a spoonful of salt, and set it on the stove to heat. Get out two small double-boilers, put the tomato sauce in one, the meat sauce in the other, and put *them* on to heat. Go in the dining room and set your table. Set out wine glasses, and open a bottle of red ink—Italian Chianti, or just as good and a lot cheaper, California Chianti, such a brand as Tipo or Cresta Bianca. Set out plates. Set out your grated cheese, and don't be stingy with it. You'll be surprised how much cheese they dump on spaghetti. Set out forks. Get ready the dishes that are to hold the sauces.

When the water boils, get out your spaghetti. Experience will have to tell you how much: a bunch the size of your arm will serve five or six people. Don't break it. Keep it together in a bunch, and souse the end of it into the water. In a few seconds, the part under water will soften, so you can push more under water, and in a minute or so it will all be under. See that you curl it neatly, so the strands stay parallel and the whole mass nests down in a circle. When the water boils up, cut it down to a simmer so the spaghetti won't get torn up, and note the time.

At the end of five minutes turn the sauces out into their dishes, set them on the dining room table, and call your guests. Have each guest bring his plate *right out into the kitchen*. Now is the time to take up the matter of individual preference. Those who like it *al dente,* or tough, get theirs first. Depending on the size of spaghetti you use, their portions will be ready at the end of six or seven minutes of cooking. The medium contingent comes next, say at the end of seven and a half or eight minutes of cooking. The well-doners come last, but eight to nine minutes will be plenty, even for them. In event you have a novice on your hands, who expresses no preference, give it to him well done. Only a real spaghetti hound, with years of experience behind him, likes it *al dente.* Make each guest hold his own plate, right over next to the pot, while you hook it out in the manner set forth above. As soon as they have their spaghetti, send them into the dining room, for spaghetti cools faster than anything on earth. Let each guest apply sauce as he likes. There is always one peculiar fellow, the same one who always puts salt in his beer, who like his with butter only. What is left, leave right in the water for second helping. It will be a little soft, but if you run the water out of the pot, the hot metal will cause it to stick, and softness is better than stickiness.

Now the sauces, if you are foolish enough to try them. The big hazard is burning them, which ruins them completely. So cook slowly at all times, and stir them constantly. You can't use double boilers, or the job will take you all day, though these are absolutely essential when you re-heat them to serve.

From *Fit For a King*
by Merle Armitage
Longman Green 1939

## Recipe: Midnight Spaghetti sauces

*Meat*
1 cup onions, finely chopped
1 cup carrots, finely chopped
1 cup celery, finely chopped
4 cups ground beef: this must be lean meat, finely ground
1 pint good Burgundy
2 quarts heavy beef broth or beef stock
Fry the onions, carrots and celery together in sweet butter, to a golden brown. Add the meat, cook together for about 10 minutes. Add the burgundy, cook a half hour, add the beef broth, cook one hour. Salt to taste. When finished, store in jars in icebox. Heat in double boiler.

*Tomato*
6 tomatoes, finely chopped, including the juice
1 onion, sliced
1 celery stalk, cut to pieces
1 carrot, sliced
1 whole black pepper
1 ham bone
Cook together slowly, two or three hours, in the juice of tomatoes to a puree. Take out ham bone and strain. Salt to taste.

# D ESSERTS

□□□□□□□□□□□□□□□□□□□□□□□□

## *Cake and Courage*

*W*hen she heard the car back out of the garage, she gave a low, *frightened exclamation, and ran to the window. They used it so seldom now, except on Sundays if they had a little money to buy gas, that she had completely forgotten about it. And so, as she saw this man slip out of her life, the only clear thought in her head was that now she had no way to deliver the cake.*

*She had got the last rosebud in place, and was removing stray flecks of icing with a cotton swab wound on a toothpick, when there was a rap on the screen door, and Mrs. Gessler, who lived next door, came in. She was a thin, dark woman of forty or so, with lines on her face that might have come from care, and might have come from liquor. Her husband was in the trucking business, but they were more prosperous than most truckers were at that time. There was a general impression that Gessler trucks often dropped down to Point Loma, where certain low, fast boats put into the cove.*

*Seeing the cake, Mrs. Gessler gave an exclamation, and came over to look. It was indeed worth the stare which her beady eyes gave it. All its decorations were now in place, but in spite of their somewhat conventional design, it had an aroma, a texture, a totality that proclaimed high distinction. It carried on its face the guarantee that every crumb would meet the inexorable confectioners' test: It must melt on the tongue.*

*In an awed way, Mrs. Gessler murmured: "I don't see how you do it, Mildred. It's beautiful, just beautiful."*
  *"If you have to do it, you can do it."*
  *"But it's* beautiful!"

from Mildred Pierce

# Square Doughnuts

In Boston a company has announced that it will manufacture square doughnuts, and we wish to say that we are flatly and unconditionally opposed to this innovation. Since the foundation of our Republic in the year 1789, it has been the right of the American people to have round doughnuts, and any movement to supply them with square doughnuts must be regarded as an outrageous subversion of civil liberties. We have our suspicions as to where this invention started. We prefer to reserve these for future publication, but we will say this much now: square doughnuts smack of cubist art, and cubist art, as we all know, originates in Moscow, and is part of the insidious Communist propaganda to overthrow our Government and fly the red flag over the Capitol. It is said that a patent has been applied for in connection with square doughnuts, and we earnestly beseech the Patent Office not to allow the corporate seal of the United States to be used in this connection. If things get much worse, they will be selling us doughnuts without any holes in them!

New York World editorial<br>June 27, 1926

# Cantaloupes

The first cantaloupes of the season, it is announced have arrived from Mexico. Wherefore we beg leave to say that we are not interested.

The cantaloupe under ideal conditions is unquestionably the finest melon ever grown. If it is pulled dead ripe after a period of dry weather, so that no rain has got into it to make it watery and tasteless; if, after it is pulled, it is placed in a cool springhouse for a few hours to bring it to the proper temperature; if, after it has been cooled and cut, no ice is allowed to touch it and absorb its flavor and benumb its perfume, then it is truly incomparable. But if these conditions are not met it is hardly fit to eat. For in proportion as it is delicate in its impact on the senses, it is also delicate in constitution; let a single adverse factor be present, and it pines, languishes and gives up the ghost, becoming a thing of so much rind and pulp.

Unfortunately for us who live in New York, it is the victim of almost every conceivable adverse factor before it reaches us. It is pulled green, with no regard to the weather that has gone before. It is shipped North in refrigerator cars which all but freeze it on its journey. It is rolled out in crates for the inspection of commission men, and then hauled to steaming markets which all but cook it while it waits on sidewalks. It is pawed over by buyers for hotels, restaurants and lunch-rooms and presently lands in a smelly kitchen, in company with a bushel of onions. Finally it is cut and packed with ice. And by the time it reaches your plate it is a sorry thing to behold. Its once firm meat has degenerated to a soft squashiness on the inside, and a hard fibrousness on the outside. As soon as you try to eat it the soft part comes off in layers. And if you do take a mouthful you find that it has no more flavor than a turnip.

Thus we may be pardoned if we regard the first shipment of Mexican cantaloupes as something less than an occasion for rejoicing. The only melon for a New Yorker to eat is a honeydew. It is no great shakes of a melon to start out with, hardly to be mentioned in the same breath with a cantaloupe. But it is rugged. You can freeze it, thaw it, play football with it, and you can't hurt it. It is the same melon when you get it as it was when it left the patch. So here's to it. It is the Tom Heeney of melons.

*New York World* editorial
April 16, 1928

# Lemon Tree

Of all the things that we might miss in that house that we left a fortnight ago when we up-anchored and moved nine miles to Hollywood, the only thing that we actually do miss is the lemon tree. To me, at any rate, it was a strange kind of thing to have in the back yard. I had always thought of lemons as coming from queer and improbable places and was never certain whether they grew on vines, like cantaloupes, or were dug out of the ground, like potatoes.

Well, they grow on a tree, and whenever we needed a lemon we just went out there and picked it. It wasn't at all like that dreary picture you conjure up when somebody hands you this one: "Of course, we have our own milk, and our radishes, lettuce, parsley, and all those things come straight from the garden to the table, so *fresh* you'd hardly believe it, and the *corn,* oh, my, you've never *tasted* corn until you've had it pulled right from the stalk and put in the pot twenty minutes before meal-time—it's so delicious, so *delicious.*"

That kind of thing is an awful headache, for the cow, of course, has to be pastured, washed and milked; the radishes, lettuce and parsley have to be weeded, and the corn planted, hoed and thinned—the very idea of all this is horrible to me. Our lemon tree was nothing like that. It was a sort of Lewis Carroll lemon tree: you went out and picked a lemon, and that was all you did about it. It flowered all year long and bore all year long: there was always one lemon particularly big, bright and yellow, and that was the one you took. Also, it was an aid to thought. I would lie there and look at it, and as soon as the hummingbird showed up I would have an idea for an article.

Now we haven't any lemons, we haven't any hummingbirds, and I haven't any ideas. All we got in exchange was a mint bed. So I suppose, for the duration of the lease, I shall be shaving ice, dissolving sugar, plucking mint, and making my friends a mint julep, that horrible drink. Mint julep, like sparkling Burgundy, was invented by novelists, not by bartenders.

Well, I am going to insult them all. I am going to put a cherry on top of it. If I only had my lemon tree back I would make them a whisky sour, a really superior drink.

Hearst column
November 12, 1934

# Oh Les Crêpes Suzettes

Brother, it's none of my business why you want to make *crêpes suzettes*, but you can't blame me for having my suspicions about it. In the first place, you're not going to serve them at a dinner for eight, for your kitchen will be inadequate no matter how big it is and your staff will be swamped no matter how many extra boys you put into white coats to help out.

It is heresy to say so, and no doubt hurts the elegant tone of the article, but at a certain stage of the proceedings a *crêpe suzette* is indistinguishable from a flapjack, except that it is a peculiarly troublesome flapjack; if you think that you can fry twenty-four flapjacks all at once, pile them so they don't stick together, get them to the table hot, peel them off one at a time and subject them to the special operations involved—if you think you can fill this tedious business with witty talk and keep your party from dying in its chairs, you are mistaken, and you will find out to your sorrow if you try it. *Crêpes suzettes* are for one, or at most two, and if you attempt quantity production with them, you are sunk and will wish you hadn't.

In the second place, you are not going to try them until the cook has gone home, the kitchen is cleaned up and an atmosphere of quiet, suitable to scientific manipulation, has descended on the place. I warn you once more that you can't wish this job, or any part of it, off on the cook. It is too fussy, too precise, too alien to her usual method of doing things, to trust her with it. She may do it, if she has to, but she will be sure to corrupt it with baking soda or whipped cream or parsley or some other thing to which she commonly pins her somewhat naive faith, so that it will have an amateurish, tea-roomy look to it, and you will be disgraced. You does this job yourself if you want it to come off, and as it is no very expensive job once you have stocked the paraphernalia you need, I advise you to practice it quite a bit in secret, so you can do it with an air, before you attempt it before a witness.

And in the last place, you are hardly going to offer this dish to a gentleman friend. He is much better pleased with beer and a Swiss-on-rye, and it is useless for you to tell me you are going to offer it to him anyhow, just because you like him. I won't believe you. *Crêpes suzettes,* as you know and I know and we all know, are for the feminine gender, and there is no use in your trying to hand me any apple-sauce about it. They flatter the feminine gender in an elusive yet undeniable way; they reach its heart, or what it laughingly refers to as a heart, as orchids reach it and summer ermine reaches it; they make it feel it is loved for itself alone and not for certain other things that it is vain of but reticent about. They amuse it. They make it clap its hands. They make it amiable, docile and friendly.

This leaves you, as well as I can make out, at the hour of midnight, with a member of the feminine gender sitting not far away, the fire stoked up and the lights stoked down, and *crêpes suzettes* on your mind. As I say, what she is doing in your apartment in the first place, what gave you this idea of *crêpes suzettes,* what your intentions are after she has gobbled the dish—these things are none of my business. They hire me to tell you how to make the cakes, not to make dirty cracks about your conduct. However, this is what I am getting at: It would be just as well if you didn't write me any letters, with stamped, self-addressed envelope enclosed, asking for further elucidation of some point I didn't quite make clear. You might give yourself away. I shall make everything clear, don't worry about that. Indeed, the whole thing is so clear by now that I am beginning to wonder whether it ought to be printed at all.

You goes out, then, and you shops yourself up some supplies. A chafing dish is indispensable to this rite: in fact, it is the foundation of it. If you have followed these pieces, you should have the proper chafing dish by now: if not, get a plain one with an alcohol lamp under it whose flame you can control, that is, that you can reduce or increase with the turn of a handle. Don't let anybody sell you an electric chafing dish for this purpose. The chief charm of *crêpes suzettes,* to the feminine eye, is the amount of blue flame they involve, and as a preliminary statement of the *motif,* the alcohol flame is highly desirable.

Next, get a smallish, silver-plated platter. This is used on the frame of the chafing dish instead of the dish itself. It should be small enough to rest easily on the frame and deep enough to hold quite a little sauce without slopping it around.

Next, get a pan for frying the *crêpes,* or better still, since they don't cost much, four pans, one for each burner of your gas stove so you can fry four cakes at the same time and serve them hot. Get these pans preferably at a restaurant supply house. They are small, japanned frying pans, very shallow. They should be five or six inches across the bottom, no bigger. Once you get them never wash them. Wipe them out after each using, and put them away. They improve with time.

Get a flat, thin knife, blunt or rounded at the end, and as flexible as you can find. This is for turning the cakes. Some flapjacks you can turn by pitching them up in the air and others by using a cake turner, but not these babies. They are temperamental cakes, and the only way I know that you can turn them without tearing them to pieces is with the same flat, thin, blunt and flexible knife.

This, regardless of what you hear of its closely guarded and almost incomprehensible mysteries, is not in the least difficult. Take four lumps of sugar. Rub two of them against an orange and two of them against a lemon. When the skins are well grated into the sugar, crack them up a little and put them into an ordinary small pan. To them add a good-sized lump of butter, a jigger of Cointreau and a jigger of Benedictine. Light the gas and melt all this together. Don't boil it and don't scorch it. Just coddle it along until it is melted into an even mixture. When it is done, pour it into a cruet, a gravy boat or some faintly improbable container. I suggest you peer at it closely, and mutter to yourself over it, as though it were a brew of inordinate complexity. This won't make it better, but it will make it seem better. I suggest, too, that you don't encourage any undue familiarity on her part during these preliminaries, which perforce have to take place in the kitchen. She will probably want to peer at everything very closely, and she may offer to do something, such as preparing the sugar: discourage her, politely but coldly. It is part of her nature, at the end, to steal your act and begin talking about *our crêpes suzettes*; for my part, I find this annoying and I think that she should be made to keep her place.

Rapt concentration is the proper note in the kitchen, the attitude of a maestro who is doing something so delicate he just can't bother with little girls till later.

Next, mix the batter for your cakes. Into a small pitcher break an egg and pour in a cup of milk. Mix the egg and the milk together with a spoon. Add flour and keep stirring until you have a thin batter. As to exactly *how* thin you will have to learn with a little practice. The cakes should be as thin as you can possibly get them without having them fall into shreds as soon as you touch them, and of course, the thinner the batter the thinner the cakes. But as I have said, you will have to do some work in secret to get this down pat.

With your batter mixed, wipe your *crêpe* pans lightly but thoroughly with butter, put them on the burners with the gas turned low and let them heat a little, but not too much. While they are heating, warm a plate. Now then, pour your cakes. They should just cover the bottom of the pans, starting up the sides. It is a good idea to pause briefly between pans, so the cakes don't all cook at the same time, else they may have you hopping around pretty lively. As soon as the first cake is done on the bottom, run the flexible knife under it and turn it. Do this carefully, or it will tear and you will have to throw it away. As to when it is done, I can't tell you very clearly. You will have to learn by experience. Small blisters appear on it, for one thing, and the top begins to look quite dry. As soon as Cake No. 1 is turned, turn the others. Let them cook a little, and then with the knife, put them carefully, one on top of the other, on the warm plate. Pour four more. They cook quite rapidly once you get started and it might be a good idea, just to show you do things in a big way, to make an even dozen.

All right, your sauce is ready and a dozen cakes are on the plate. Put the chafing dish frame, with the lamp ready, the cakes, the sauce, the silver platter, knives, forks, plates, and a bottle of cognac, on a tray, go into the living-room with it and park it on the low table in front of the fireplace. Have her go ahead and open doors for you: this will keep her from sticking her finger in the sauce although she had probably done this already.

Light the lamp. Put the platter on the frame of the chafing dish so it heats a little. Pour into it the sauce. Now, with a knife and fork, take the top cake and fold it neatly, twice. That is, fold it so a quarter section is showing. Do not roll the cake. You roll French pancakes, which is an entirely different dish. Fold it neatly, put it on the platter and sop it thoroughly in the sauce. Then push it still folded neatly, up toward the end. A good head waiter usually unfolds the cake while sopping it in the sauce, then refolds it, but if I were you I wouldn't bother with this or you are likely to pull all your cakes to pieces.

Proceed in the same way with the rest of your cakes, unless you find that you have too many cakes for the sauce, in which case let the rest of them go. Pile each cake neatly against the one before, so that when you are done, they look like so many folded handkerchiefs running down the length of the platter, with quite a little sauce swimming around their edges. Now then, pour on a good generous jigger of cognac and cut your room lights. Light the cognac. While it is still burning, serve her four or five cakes on her plate and hand them to her. Of course, they would taste better if you let the cognac burn itself out before you served them, but such is her nature that she likes to "blow out the fire" on her plate, so you had better have a little on it for her to blow out.

Serve your own plate. Smack your lips. Make one or two technical criticisms. Be evasive as to where you learned the art. Sit back. Look at her. Forget to turn on the lights. Estimate your chances. If you have done it right you ought to rate an even break.

*Esquire*, February 1935

# Recipe: Oh Les Crêpes Suzette

*Necessary utensils:* 1 chafing dish with alcohol lamp; 4 small, very shallow frying pans (so that you can cook 4 crêpes at once on your stove); a silver-plated platter to be used on the frame of the chafing dish, instead of the dish itself. Should be deep enough to hold quite a bit of sauce; a flat, thin knife blunt or rounded at the end.

Take four lumps of sugar, rub two of them against an orange, two of them against a lemon. When the skins are well grated into the sugar, crack them up and put them into an ordinary pan. Add 1 lump of butter, a jigger of Cointreau and a jigger of Benedictine. Light the gas and melt all this together. Do not boil or scorch. When it is done, pour into a gravy dish, muttering over it to yourself as if it were a brew of inordinate complexity.

*The batter:* Into a small pitcher, break an egg and pour in a cup of milk. Stir until you have a thin batter, the thinner the batter the better. Wipe your 4 crêpe pans lightly with butter, let them heat for a minute on the burners with gas turned low. Pour your cakes; they should just cover the bottom of the pan. Stagger pouring so the crepes are not all cooking at exactly the same time. When the first cake is done, turn it carefully with the flexible knife. Let it cook a little, then with knife carefully place it on a warmed plate. Pour 4 more crêpes and repeat procedure. A dozen is a good serving for 2 people. Place a few crêpes, neatly folded and sopped in the sauce, on a warm plate; cover them with Cognac, dim light and light Cognac. Good luck.

# II

# GUIDE TO
# HOME SINGING
# AND SINGERS

"*I think much about beauty, sitting alone at night, listening to my wireless, and trying to get the reason of it, and understand how a man like Strauss can put the worst sounds on the surface that ever profaned the night, and yet give me something I can sink my teeth into. This much I know: True beauty has terror in it. Now I shall reply to your contemptuous words about Beethoven. He has terror in him, and your overture writers have not. Fine music they wrote, and after your remarks I shall listen to them with respect. But you can drop a stone into Beethoven, and you will never hear it strike bottom. The eternities and the infinities are in it, and they strike at the soul, like death. You mind what I'm telling you, there is terror in the little one too, and I hope you never forget it in your relations with her."*

*There wasn't much I could say to that. I had felt the terror in her, God knows. We lit up again, and watched Ensenada turn gray, blue and violet. My cigarettes were all gone by then, and I was smoking his tobacco, and one of his pipes, that he had cleaned out for me on a steam jet in the boiler. Not a hundred feet from the ship a black fin lifted out of the water. It was an ugly thing to see. It was at least thirty inches high, and it didn't zigzag, or cut a V in the water, or any of the things it does in books. It just came up and stayed a few seconds. Then there was the swash of a big tail and it went down.*

*"Did you see it, lad?"*

*"God, it was an awful-looking thing, wasn't it?"*

*"It cleared up for me what I've been trying to say to you. Sit here, now, and look. The water, the surf, the colors on the shore. You think they make the beauty of the tropical sea, aye, lad? They do not. 'Tis the knowledge of what lurks below the surface of it, that awful-looking thing, as*

*you call it, that carries death with every move that it makes.*
*So it is, so it is with all beauty."*

from *Serenade*

# INTRODUCTION

□□□□□□□□□□□□□□□□□□□□□□□□□

ames M. Cain's love of music and singing went back to his childhood. His mother was an accomplished vocalist who gave up a promising opera career to marry a Yale man she was in love with. For a brief time when he was around 20, Cain flirted with the idea of becoming an opera singer. But after a summer of music lessons and discouraged by his mother (who did not think he had either the voice or the temperament to sing grand opera), he decided against a musical career. But he never gave up his love of music or singing. And music—like sex and food—was part of the creative mix that produced Cain's novels. In addition to *Career in C Major,* there is *Serenade,* about an opera singer, *Mildred Pierce,* concerned with raising a child singing star, and *The Moth,* a picturesque novel about a boy soprano coming of age in the Depression. All his novels which have music as an underlying theme, or involve singers, are, said Cain, "wreaths laid at my mother's grave."

It has also been pointed out that Cain's novels themselves were musical in their structure and that he usually brought them to a climax the way a composer develops a coda. And Cain acknowledged this to the extent that he agreed that the novels which adhered to a theme—*The Postman, Past All Dishonor, The Butterfly* and *Double Indemnity*—were his biggest hits. "My tastes in music are thematic, not programmatic," he wrote one student of his writing. "Beethoven, Mendelssohn, Puccini, Mascagni, Bizet, and such men are my favorites, all different emotionally, but similar in the logic of their musical approach. Wagner, Richard Strauss, Debussy and such men who depend on an overpowering gush of tone, harmony and color tend to bore me. It even carries over to the popular side, for Vincent Youmans interests me more than any American composer, as he is the only one that I know of who makes tunes out of themes, as such. 'Tea for Two' is a thematic building of tune out of three notes treated as a theme. It therefore, to my imagination, is exciting, all the more so because of its leanness."

Cain's writing on music started early, when he was working for the *Baltimore Sun*. One of his first by-lined pieces appeared on the op ed page in 1922, and deplored the then current boom in America for Gilbert and Sullivan. Cain charged in, attacking English music in general, and Gilbert and Sullivan comedies in particular, advising the song writers around the country who were imitating the British musical comedy team to try something exciting—like jazz. Music was also one of his favorite subjects when he was Walter Lippmann's "human interest" writer on the editorial page of *The New York World,* as well as when he wrote his syndicated column for the Hearst papers in the early 1930s. A few of these editorials and columns are included here, just for the record.

Cain himself had what he called a barroom bass. Ruth Goodman Goetz, the playwright, was a young girl in the 1920s when Cain would come around to her house with H. L. Mencken to visit her father, Philip Goodman. "The first time I remember hearing anything out of him," she recalled, when I interviewed her for my biography of Cain, "was when my mother was playing the piano, some Debussy, and from the other side of the room came a voice singing. My father, astonished, said: 'Jim, you sing?' and he said 'Yes.' My mother said 'Can I play something you'd like to sing?' and he said: 'You got any Sibelius?' My mother said: 'No,' but father asked: 'If we got some Sibelius, will you sing?' He said 'yes' and from then on, whenever he came to our house he would sing. He had a quite lovely voice and it was obvious he had some training."

Cain's enjoyment of musical evenings in the home reached a crescendo in the mid-1930s, after *The Postman* was published and the Cains moved from Burbank back into Hollywood and their large, attractive home on Belden Drive. One of his Hollywood friends was Henry Meyers, a playwright who had worked on the scripts for "Million Dollar Legs" and "Destry Rides Again." Meyers, like Cain, was a music enthusiast who could sight read and play almost anything on the piano. One night, Cain and Meyers were talking about music and deploring the fact that people did not play instruments or sing in their homes as they used to do before the radio and phonographs began to dominate family life. But they decided human nature had not changed and that, given a chance, people would step forward and, if nothing else, display their exhibitionism. They decided to organize musical evenings every Friday night at the Cain house—and the results were so successful that Cain wrote an article about the evenings for *The Mercury* (see "Close Harmony").

According to one friend who attended the evening, Cain was "a darling host," and before long they had a huge chorus. The regulars, in addition to Cain and Meyers, who played the piano, were the Raphaelsons, Dorothy Speare, a writer who had once sung opera, Gertrude Purcell, a former Ziegfeld girl, then a screenwriter who worked on "Destry Rides Again" with Meyers, Jay Gorney, the composer who wrote music for "The Wizard of Oz," and a San Francisco Opera baritone, Mostyn Thomas. One night Franson Manson, a Columbia Studios story editor, was invited providing she brought a tenor. When a story conference prevented her from attending, she sent her tenor along with Jo Swerling, invited because his wife, Florence, was a contralto. The tenor was introduced as "Mike Swartz" by the Swerlings, who said they could not vouch for his talent. But when he opened up, Cain knew he had a tenor—and as it turned out he was right. Mike Swartz was, in reality, Michael Bartlett, recently of the Philadelphia Opera Company—in Hollywood to make "Love Me Forever" with Grace Moore. But Cain did not care. Bartlett was welcome. Anybody was welcome if he had a voice and, more important, could read music and not object to singing a part, rather than solo (although Cain himself would occasionally end the evening with a certain breezy number that began, "George Washington was the father of his country," and ended with Cain taking a handkerchief from his pocket and waving it at his audience, who more often than not would boo).

The evenings were mostly devoted to serious music, however, and it is obvious from Cain's writings and interviews that he was continuing his musical education and learning quite a bit about singers and singing. He also learned how good amateur musicians could be, at least in California, and found that if people had the opportunity, they were eager to participate in home singing. In fact, they were soon coming uninvited to the Cain Friday night festivals, in such numbers that the Cains finally had to ring down the curtains on the evenings. Cain and Meyers also found they were spending so much time locating scores and studying music that it was interfering with their work.

But the singing did make an important contribution to Cain's writing. During these evening and later when he was attending local opera, he was giving more and more thought to the timbre and quality of a man's voice and what made it different. "At last, I begin to see dimly what makes a singer good," he said. He mentioned one baritone he knew who had "a superb voice, but he really isn't any good. Well, why? I'm figuring it out, little by little . . . . This much I know: This mob has better voices than the professional mobs have, and yet they don't get there. It had something to do with that mystical thing the teachers call voice line: that is, how to hit the tone quality that a scene calls for, maintain it constantly, and develop it so it rams home the intent of the music. Sounds simple, but I can see that it isn't."

And the more he thought about the human voice, the more confidence he gained in his theory that there was a relationship between homosexuality and voice. John Lee Mahin recalled Cain's remarking at concerts "that a guy sang with his balls. And sometimes, if Cain didn't like a singer, he'd say: 'He doesn't have any balls; a guy's got to have balls.'" Cain would talk with singers about this and they would understand, especially the women. One singer in particular, Mary McCormick, became very excited about the idea and told Cain she knew exactly what he was talking about—"this peculiar color of a homo's voice," as Cain called it. He also was impressed by the fact that all the really great male singers were macho, high livers—Caruso, McCormick, etc. And he had met a male singer who told him he had such feelings of guilt about liking a man that it sometimes made a difference in his singing. "Naturally, I have no means of knowing which singers are homos, but it is not too difficult to hazard a guess, from their appearance, walk, manners, etc., which might be, or at least if not outright a hundred percent, would have a leaning in that direction." With these men he thought it was easy to detect what Juanita, the Mexican whore in the novel he would write someday, would identify as an absence of "toro." And he knew he would write the novel now because not only did his associations with singers help convince him he was on to a significant fact, but one night at the Raphaelsons' he had met a prominent Los Angeles physician, Dr. Samuel Hirshfeld, to whom he told the story about the singer and the Mexican whore. Dr. Hirshfeld wanted to know why he had not written it, and Cain gave his usual reply, "Oh, I don't know—I just don't care to write a book a doctor would laugh at."

"Well, I'm not laughing," said Hirshfeld, "I'm hanging on the edge of my seat." And then for an hour he described the importance of voice in a doctor's diagnosis and how much attention a doctor pays to it. Dr. Hirshfeld's endorsement was all Cain needed. He decided the time had come to write the novel that would eventually be titled *Serenade*.

One of the divinities of Cain's youth was the Minnesota opera star, Florence Macbeth. But he did not meet her until 1945 in Hollywood, just after he had separated from his third wife, the movie star Ailene Pringle. He and Florence fell immediately in love, were married in 1946 and he spent the next 20 years happily married to Florence, although he never did hear her sing—except on phonograph records. Cain, of course, never lost his interest in singers and singing and in his twilight years, while living in Hyattsville, Maryland, he wrote a few articles on music, including one on his favorite subject—that the "Star Spangled Banner" can be sung if you do it in the right key.

As his lifelong friend, Samuel Raphaelson, said in a tribute to Cain read at his memorial service: "He was a man of music. Almost every paragraph of his was the complex product of an orchestral inner ear."

# GUIDE TO HOME
# SINGING AND SINGERS

□□□□□□□□□□□□□□□□□□□□□□□

## Close Harmony

You are familiar, no doubt, with the lament that people don't make music any more; that what they do is sit around and listen to it, on the radio, the phonograph, or some other device that gives it to them canned, without effort to themselves. Indeed, if you believe the American Society of Composers, Authors, and Publishers, this state of affairs has become a national calamity, with sales of sheet music reduced to pitiful figures, and that sturdy home group, consisting of Brother, with his violin, Father, with his cornet, and Sister, at the piano, vanished from the scene, never to return. Well, I used to discuss this with a friend, Henry Myers, the playwright, and he felt, as I did, that it was deplorable. And then one night we did an about-face, and decided it was all nonsense. The human race can't have changed overnight, we said. Nowadays, people have no way to make music, yet given the chance, they would betray their natural exhibitionism now as of yore and for aye. So we decided to try an experiment. We would actually try to make some music, and see what happened.

So we started out. We got some music and rounded up some singers. We set Friday night of each week for the outcry, and warned neighbors to chain up the dogs. We spit on our hands and promised to mean it. I give you one guess how it turned out. We made so much music that it snowed us under; we got so tied up with duets, trios, and solos with chorus that we couldn't work, and it got so bad after a while that in self-defense we had to ring down the curtain, so we could make our livings. We proved our theory all right, with plenty to spare. But that wasn't all we did. We found out a few things about music, and some of them may interest you.

How, for example, does music stand up when homemade in this way? We may grant at once that the ultimate test of it is the test of the jungle: what it sounds like when played by professionals, how it weathers time, how it wins a place in repertoire, how it holds that place. But this other test, the one you make in your own home, has a certain validity too. It is rather hard, perhaps, if you have never taken part in such a rite, to understand the excitement that takes hold of you when you do good music, the sense of accomplishment that you get when you have mastered it, the feeling that comes to you after a whole evening of it, of having stood in the shadows of great edifices, of having identified yourself with something that was pointed at the stars. There is no particular awe mixed up with it; it is not like being in church, and you don't see any particular eye-rolling on the part of the performers, or rhapsodical outbursts of any kind. It is comparable, I should say, with eating a good dinner, and drinking with it a great wine, as distinguished from merely a good wine; there is a sense of becoming a part of positive beauty, something beyond words, something that can be felt alongside the most commonplace celebration, and the most casual talk.

It eliminates certain factors, too, which greatly corrupt your judgment of music when you merely listen to it, as for example the entertainment coefficient. Music is subject to this, as drama is, and literature, and everything else. You sit in a theater, and you hear John Charles Thomas sing the *Pagliacci* Prologue, and you clap wildly, probably under the impression that you are applauding music. But what you are really applauding is lights, costumes, orchestra, smart rendition, and Thomas's A flat. When you try *Pagliacci* in your home, and regard it from the inside-looking-out instead of from the outside-looking-in, you discover in short order what a piece of claptrap it really is, for it gives you none of that feeling I was just talking about. It is valid theatrically, that is as entertainment, but it is almost worthless musically. In your home, you see, entertainment doesn't entertain. Nobody comes there to clown, to put on an act, to bring down applause. What they come for is just what I spoke of: that sense of accomplishment, that excitement in the presence of greatness, that feeling that what was done was worth doing—and that is all they come for. There is no audience, except a few kibitzers sitting around. There is no show going on next week. There is nothing that makes entertainment, as such, an object. Music, in your home, must win as music, and as nothing else.

And it brings into the open certain factors that you would never become aware of in a million years of just listening to music. Singers are a peculiar breed. They will take all sorts of care, submit to the most gruelling punishment, simply to get something right, provided they feel it is worth it. If they don't feel it is worth it, they won't take any care at all, and you had just as well quit trying to make them take care. They would take care, of course, if you were paying them; but if you are not, and the only reward in store for them is the music itself, then the music had better be good if you want to get any work out of them. It is the chance to observe this factor at work, I think, that is one of the main values of home music, and that eventually will cause you to revise many of your previous estimates of music, regardless of how dearly those previous estimates were cherished.

The biggest surprise we got was the indifferent quality of the music of Arthur Sullivan. Like everybody else, we were going to do Gilbert and Sullivan, and like everybody else, once we got started with it we were grievously disappointed. The main thing to remember here is that Sullivan, regardless of how simple he sounds in the theater, is very difficulty to execute. He is not difficult vocally, for while the range of his arias is tolerably wide, the *tessitura* is comfortable, and he had an instinct for melodies that are singable. He is difficult musically. He disliked the obvious, and he had the technical equipment to avoid the obvious; this led him into musical syntax that was intricate, to say the least. Literally, there is hardly a number in all these operas that does not involve some tricky piano cue, some left-handed bit of harmony, some improbable rhythm, that makes rendition hard. Such roles, for example, as Ko-Ko, Deadeye, and the Lord Chancellor, that sound so simple, and that you probably associate with clowns rather than singers, are in reality not simple at all. The Lord Chancellor, even in the jigging number he sings on his entrance, has an accompaniment that will throw him out of step unless he glues his eyes on the conductor; in the finale of Act I he has intervals so arbitrary that I have yet to hear him sing completely in key; in the trio in Act II he has a couple of measures of deceptive tonality; as for the Nightmare Song, it is truly a nightmare, and I wonder he ever gets through it at all.

To sing Sullivan requires hard work, and plenty of it, and after you put that much work on it you are pretty clearly aware of what you've got. Well, what have you got? So far as we were concerned, we had a most pretentiously designed cream-puff. It seemed almost impossible for us really to get our minds on this stuff and lick it; we just couldn't make ourselves take pains with it. We took pains with other things, but not with this. And even when we occasionally did take pains with it, we didn't feel it was worth it. Sullivan, I am afraid, is an over-rated man, at least by those who assume he has a musical validity in addition to his theatrical effectiveness. He simply doesn't stick to your ribs. I suspect that really he was a function of Gilbert, and that secretly he knew it, as some of his correspondence indicates. When Gilbert was good, Sullivan was good; when Gilbert was bad, he was bad; when Gilbert wasn't there at all, Sullivan didn't exist, as his symphonies, and such things as *Ivanhoe,* readily attest.

If Sullivan turned out to be a turkey, it would be most unkind to say what his colleagues of the same faculty turned out to be. For many years, I had been one of the light opera boys; I was most impatient with those who sniffed at music merely because it was light; indeed, I seem to remember myself saying, "There's more music in *The Merry Widow* than there is in most grand opera,"—and I really believed this. Unfortunately, it isn't true. There just ain't no music in *The Merry Widow* at all. It sounds swell when you are half full of beer, and Lüchow's orchestra plays it; but when you get in there with it, it merely sounds sick. I got it, and *Robin Hood,* and *The Chimes of Normandy,* and thought we would do one of them when we were a little tired of Sullivan. We tried them over, and I got cured. What is it about these things that makes them seem so charming when presented, and that crumbles and blows away when you move up close to them? I don't know. It is like those short stories that seem so sensational when they come out illustrated, in some magazine; reprinted, between covers, they are absurd. These things, in the various arts, are produced by men with great talent and no brains; with the gift of speech, they have nothing to say. The futility of glibness strikes home to you when you repeat after them, and say their platitudes yourself.

## II

If music of this kind doesn't repay your efforts, then what music does?

I am sorry to disappoint you if you have been hoping for some recondite titles that nobody has thought of before, but I am afraid I shall have to. The music that stands up, when you are spending your own sweat on it, is that same music you have heard about all your life, and somehow forgotten. You can trot out your old English folk songs, your German *lieder,* your transcriptions from the Ukranian, your four-part arrangements of the worthy Negro's efforts, and very pretty they will all sound, very worth your trouble they will be; but when it comes to something to sink your teeth into, you will sing Mozart, Handel, Haydn, Bach, Brahms, Beethoven, Mendelssohn, Palestrina, and the Scarlattis, together with their lesser heirs and assigns, and that is about all you will sing. They still rule the roost. There is an impression they do not, since grand opera became fashionable; this impression is wrong. If light opera, on rendition, turns out to be molasses, grand opera turns out to be molasses and sulphur, a most unpleasant dose. We tried numbers from *Traviata, Trovatore, Faust, Martha, Aïda,* and no doubt others: of the result, the less said the better. The strangest flop was Puccini. He is beloved, of course, by tenors and sopranos, and our performers had to give him a whirl. Their efforts were appalling, and it wasn't entirely the way they did it. So far as I can make out, there is simply nothing in Puccini. The biggest part of him, I suspect, is his orchestra. It plays on your ears sensuously, rather than musically, lulls your critical sense, and obscures the tripey essence of the show. But this orchestra, when transcribed for piano, sounds God-awful. You may say it was not supposed to be transcribed for piano; and so saying, you will be wrong. Music, whether played by orchestra, piano, or harmonica, should have some inner core of beauty that survives any rendition. All you can say about Puccini is that he is another Sullivan, effective in the theater, and no place else: subtract the tenors, the violins, the lights, the paint, and the tears, and there is nothing left.

Our great discovery was Rossini. Friends, there's a man. We had a soprano with a superb voice; it wasn't oppressively big, but it had that curious quality called "noble" by the critics and "rich" by the teachers, that made it suitable for heroic stuff. So I got her the *Inflammatus* from the *Stabat Mater.* When she stepped into the G that opens it, the effect on the rest was electrical. When she had ripped off the strain beginning *"Inflammatus et accensus,"* there was no more chance that they would fall down on the chorus part of the number than that they would go home without their hats. And they didn't. We filed, sandpapered, and polished on that number until it became, as Henry said, our "masterpiece."

Then, having done so well on that, we decided to see what the rest of the mass looked like. It turned out to be a veritable gold mine, and we dug into it hard. You understand: Rossini is even more difficult than Sullivan. He isn't musically as difficult, for where Sullivan wrote the obvious with a hocus-pocus of originality, Rossini wrote the original with a hocus-pocus of obviousness. Having no secret shame over his material, he didn't have to trick it up to make it look good; thus his idiom is clear, natural, and simple. But he is vocally formidable. His range is even wider than Sullivan's, and his *tessitura* lies high; like all Italians, he assumed that singers can sing. The *Cujus Animam,* for example, goes to D flat in alt; that is, to D flat above high C, and presents breath problems that can hardly be worked out without the aid of logarithms. That didn't feaze our tenor. He could sing a D flat in alt: as for the breath problems, he kept at them until he solved them, one after the other. Every night he arrived with the thing in a little better shape, and after a while he had it: he did credit to us all. The choruses were difficult, because they were true *andantes,* something very difficult for amateurs, and something, by the way, that Sullivan seemed unable to write. But we licked them. We worked on them until you could feel their pulse, even during the rests, and I have yet to hear a complaint about the number of times we had to go over them.

It was our great regret that we hadn't quite mastered it all when we suspended operations. Well, this is what I am getting at: with hard work required for practically everything we attempted, what we were willing to work on was something that was musically worth while. And that, I suppose, is why *The Messiah, The Creation,* the *Missa Solemnis,* the Bach *B Minor,* and perhaps half a dozen other works of a similar kind, supply choruses with three-fourths of the music they sing, now as a hundred years ago. These things, when we are flipping through catalogues trying to decide on some new selections for our electric phonograph, usually strike us as worn, trite, hardly worth hearing any more. That is because most of us, as mere listeners to music, have become connoisseurs of novelties rather than appraisers of value. As a participant in music, one finds that these works, supposedly so familiar, are not familiar at all; what is familiar is their titles, and possibly a few strains out of them: the great body of their texts, and particularly their component parts, which have to be mastered before they can be given—these seem new, and they come as a revelation to you when you move in close and really get acquainted with them.

All of which makes me wonder whether modern music, like modern football, hasn't gone off on a completely wrong tack: that is, whether it hasn't let the ticket holders become so important that it has lost sight of the fundamentals of the game. Modern music is written for the audience, pure and simple. The idea that one could enjoy somebody like Richard Strauss while playing him is absurd. And yet I think it could be demonstrated that listening to music, as such, is downright impossible. Whether we realize it or not, we all participate in music, even when we think we are only listening to it, some of us so vividly that we cannot keep our feet still. And music which disregards this, and treats us as though we were all mind, all taste, all criticism, impatient of the slightest banality, has somehow lost its roots. It is blasé, rather than original, dazzling, rather than moving. They pay off, in this art as in all others, on what reaches the emotions, and stirs them.

Music, in its golden age, seems to have been regarded by the composers as much more of a community affair than it is now. They expected it to be more or less homemade, with home soloists and home support. The traveling orchestra, with its soloists chosen because they are a draw, was unknown; hence there was a much more general participation than we are supposed to have now. Hence the music was pretty definitely utile: it served the needs of a community, spoke to emotions that the community felt. That is, it was pretty generally religious. That didn't hurt it any. The main point is that when it got down-to-earth, as the movie people say, it had vitality, and vitality is what gets into your heart and stays there.

### III

Before I finish I think I had better pass out some tips about the home chorus, for you may be thinking about one yourself, and I can save you a lot of grief.

Be advised, then, that it is very easy to assemble people who like to sing. It is so easy, in fact, that in this very circumstance lurks a pitfall for the unwary. The first danger, what with this one who is crazy to come and that one who sang *Floradora* with the Triangle Club, is that the thing gets too big. Twenty people standing around, all with a vague yen to sing and no clear idea how to go about it, won't make much music, and what they do make won't be much good. Furthermore, most of the twenty, after the first time or two, are likely to develop dilatory notions of attendance; with so big a crowd, nobody feels any particular responsibility, so that one night there will be a handful and the next night an overflow meeting, which is annoying.

The ideal number, for an ordinary living room, is eight; that is, a double quartet. They will give enough volume, and they can sing all parts of most of the numbers attempted. The eight should consist of two sopranos, a mezzo, and a contralto; two tenors, a baritone, and a bass. It is well to have a mezzo and a baritone, for they can sing the low parts in choruses, and they can also sing G's in solos, which is important. The eight should be selected with care, and not every candidate should be accepted. I warn especially against that "musical" person who has neither voice nor experience, but who likes to sing, and is sure he will get along all right if he can stand beside somebody that knows it. This amiable oaf can wreck a whole evening. For what he is going to do is yell melody from 9 o'clock until 12; if he tries a part, he must be taught it by rote, and he will slip off it the second you take your eye away from him; he will slow up the show and make it impossible for the others to work. The singers should have pretty good voices, they should read music with reasonable ease, and they should be able to stay on a part once they are assigned to it.

The simplest rule, if you spot somebody and have to make up your mind quick, is to go entirely by the voice. It might seem that this plan is likely to assemble people with much in their throats and nothing in their heads, but actually it won't. The truth is that a good voice, with no knowledge of music to back it up, hardly exists. The person with a voice has always known he had a voice, and at one time or another he has done something about it. So if somebody speaks of a friend with a swell bass voice, it is pretty safe to call him on spec and invite him around. And if his voice is as good as reported, he is pretty sure to like good music: voices fit for grand opera aren't much intrigued by *The Isle of Capri*.

To get the eight, of the specifications desired, may take a little time; if so, time should be taken, and when they have been got, the lists should be closed. They will get better as they grow used to each other; also, they will feel it is their outfit, and not a shifting mob to which they are occasional visitors. I mean, they will acquire an identity of their own, which is vital. In addition to the eight singers, there must be an excellent accompanist, and here again care must be taken to find the right person.

A good pianist, for some reason, is usually a bad accompanist. The person who can execute a Chopin nocturne in concert style usually dislikes to play at sight; often he can't play at sight, and sometimes he has the soloist's temperament, which dislikes to submerge itself in an ensemble. Your good accompanist, as a rule, can't play a Chopin nocturne for buttons. He is a rough-and-tumble fellow who can read anything at sight, who has a good time at the piano, and pays no more attention to whether people are looking at him than a tree toad does. He is enthusiastic about his job, and is not afflicted with the caprices of boredom, japery, and fatigue that mark his more gifted brother. He has an instinct to follow performers, and can retrieve errors without letting the show crack down. He is as important as any two singers.

And there must be somebody to take charge of things and see that they get somewhere: a leader, conductor, drillmaster, or whatever you call him. But here again, care must be taken to get the right person, and possibly various members of the outfit will have to try their hands before the ultimate choice emerges. The best musicians, for some reason, don't always make the best leaders. Indeed, the musical qualifications needed here are very slight; most of them can be met by the simple strategem of learning the composition by heart, so that beating the time, cuing the parts, catching mistakes, and such things are almost automatic. What is needed is that curious impulse, felt by some people, to improve on what the composer wrote. Your good leader must have a passion for "effects"; without taking liberties with the music, he will so bring out its form, intent, and meaning that it will be something more than a set of notes correctly executed. This is important in singing, for the failure to breathe at the proper point, or to phrase well, can so blur a composition that it sounds like nothing at all.

All these people can be assembled with reasonable ease, and without coaxing professionals. It is surprising, indeed, how good amateur musicians really are, particularly amateur singers. Any local performance of *Robin Hood* will have fine voices; in our little outfit, we had voices better than most you hear in grand opera. Why they get that good and no better I don't know; it has something to do with the wide chasm that separates the amateur from the professional. But if they are that good they are good enough; my only point is that they should be that good instead of no good.

When they are assembled, the piano should be tuned at international pitch, not concert pitch. Concert pitch is so high that their throats will ache at the end of an hour, and there will be no more singing that night. There should be enough copies of the music to go round, so they don't have to peep over the pianist's shoulder. Expense, by the way, is slight. Octavo music costs from 8 to 15 cents a copy; operetta scores run around $1.50, opera scores $2.50. After the first outlay, $10 a month ought to cover the music, as one new number a night is about all that can be attempted. The social problem is nil. The various wives and husbands who show up manage to amuse themselves somehow; as for the heterogeneity of the singers, it isn't a factor. They can be sixteen or sixty, married or single, realtor or poetess, but on this lyric spot they will meet as equals, and, as long as the music lasts, get along with a cordiality most touching.

## IV

It turns out, by the way, that the crisis over mechanical music has been somewhat exaggerated. The Preeman-Matthews Company in Los Angeles, where I buy my music, assures me that they sell a great deal more choral music now than they ever did before; that the growth of amateur organizations is the main development, musically, of the past decade. The reason, it seems, is the decision of the public school systems to go in for music in a big way. Practically every high school now has its orchestra and chorus; the talent so trained wants to continue its efforts after it gets out of school, and so there have come into being many more organizations than we used to have. These range from the fifty-voice choruses of the fraternal societies, many of them doing good music, to the big 500-voice affairs that every city has nowadays. Then there are the various women's organizations, maintained in connection with clubs of various kinds, and the Parent-Teacher Associations. These last, it appears, frequently starting out to give comical programs at the meetings, often get switched over to something better; so that many a lady who thought Carrie Jacobs Bond was farthest north in classicism begins to sing Brahms, Schubert, and Sibelius. When this happens, I am assured, the lady is never the same afterwards, for a big event has taken place in her life, and she takes care that the whole world knows it.

Of course this isn't exactly home music, but it is music that occupies thousands of persons who don't get a cent for it, so things can't be hopeless. What the bottom has dropped out of is not good music, but bad music; that is, popular music, which is what the American Society of Composers, Authors, and Publishers chiefly represents.

(They rapped me for $150 once, for printing eight lines of a forgotten song in a book I wrote, so this is where I get back at them.) As for what happens to popular music, I don't care. I don't think it is the foundation course on which good music will be laid; I don't think it is anything but a bore. If the radio has killed it, robbed its confectors of the incentive to work, then all I have to say is: more power to the radio.

Well, I have achieved the feat of writing a piece which says exactly what any musician could have told me, and in point of fact, exactly what every musician *has* told me. But this much you have to admit: I tell it a lot better than they do.

*American Mercury*
October 1935

# O Say—You Can Sing It

Once again we're into the same old brouhaha, a move to junk the Star-Spangled Banner, on the ground that it is "unsingable," in favor of America the Beautiful, God Bless America, or some other favored selection, the advocates this time being a pair of congressmen, James M. Collins of Texas and Guy Vander Jagt of Michigan, surveys by various radio stations showing popular support for a change—and so, for the two-dozenth time at least, I inject myself into the discussion, on the side of the Star-Spangled Banner.

I first encountered the unsingable aspect, the allegedly unsingable aspect of our anthem, in 1913, when I was just starting a year as principal of a high school on the Eastern Shore of Maryland. I opened each day with assembly, beginning with a hymn, then a selection from the Bible, read by myself, then the Lord's Prayer, then announcements, if any. So one morning, instead of a hymn, I had the bright idea of having everyone sing the Star-Spangled Banner. The teacher who played the accompaniments didn't seem too happy about it, I had no idea why. My voice is low, and I was reading the bass part and singing along, not paying too much attention to what was going on above me. Then I noticed I was singing alone. I put this down to collective derision, a chance for a unanimous laugh at my expense, how funny I sounded. So next day, with true high-school principal's determination to show who was boss, I called for a repeat, this time keeping silent, so there'd be nothing to snicker at. But once more all voices were silent—the pianist had it all to herself, and looked up at me at the end to know if she should go on to the second verse. I shook my head no, and at last realized there was something funny about it, that our anthem couldn't be sung, that it was no perversity on the part of the kids.

That lesson stuck, and years later, when I was an editorial writer for the New York World, a prominent daily of the Twenties, I would occasionally write an editorial in favor of the Star-Spangled Banner, greatly pleasing my editor, Walter Lippmann. "I've never seen so many reasons, so many good reasons it seems to me," he told me once, "why the Star-Spangled Banner is outstanding among national anthems—I confess myself quite astonished. Not that I mind—I'm delighted, actually, to have a red-white-and-blue rainbow in the sky, especially one that seems sincere, in view of the sour note we sound so often, that we have to sound, of course, especially on the subject of Prohibition. Keep it up." Prominent among the virtues of the Star-Spangled Banner, at least as I lined them out, was the fact that it was unsingable, so it would always be played smartly, by professional band or orchestra, without a crowd dragging it out, by trying to join in, and at a brisk vivid tempo.

Then John Green got into it.

Mr. Green, Johnny Green usually known as, is the Hollywood composer, pianist, and singer, who use to have an office down the hall from me in the Thalberg Building, or Iron Lung as we called it, at M.G.M., so I count him as a friend. I was able to check with him my observations of what he did, and get his corroboration. Mr. Green had charge of the music at the Democratic Convention in Los Angeles, the one held in 1960 that nominated John F. Kennedy for President. He assembled a choir to lead the singing, composed of celebrities so dazzling they hurt your eyes, three or four dozen worthies who really could line it out. Mr. Green opened each session with the Star-Spangled delegates on the floor, and the 15,000 spectators in the balconies, to join in. To my astonishment, they did, really giving out, so it was a stirring thing to hear. But why? Why would this crowd sing, when my high school kids wouldn't? Suddenly an idea hit me, and I leaped to my piano to check Mr. Green's key. Instead of being in C, as my high school kids had been, or B-flat, as later kids were, he was in A-flat. In C the treble voice goes to G above the staff, a note so high only opera singers can sing it, and in B-flat, to F at the top of the staff, a note still too high for run-of-the-mill voices. But A-flat goes to E-flat at the top of the staff, a tone well within the range of almost anybody, and a white light dawned on me.

I'd been making a fool of myself in the World.

If Walter Lippmann had known a bit more about music, he wouldn't have been quite so pleased with the stuff I was dishing out. The Star-Spangled Banner, I was discovering, *is* unsingable when published in unsingable keys, but not when published in keys that make sense. This was explained to me by Mr. Gene Archer, who used to sing it to open Redskins football games, at first in the key of B-flat, not getting much help from the crowd. But when he switched to A-flat, they all joined in heartily, to his great satisfaction. The reason, he told me, for the use of the other keys, C at first, and then later B-flat, was that these keys are suited to military bands, which often had charge of the matter, the vocal question being disregarded.

As corroborating these general observations, there pops into my mind Miss Mildred Miller and her performance of the Star Spangled Banner one night on national television. Miss Miller, in case you don't place her, is the Metropolitan mezzo who has the distinction of being one of the few Carmens who really looked like Carmen—small, beautiful, and shapely, with a look in her eye when she wants it there. Seeing her dresed up tacky, switching her bottom in that certain way, you really believe the story, which you don't when most mezzos sing it. A fat femme fatale, alas, is a contradiction in terms, and most Carmens are fat—we could even say obese. Well, Miss Miller sang our anthem at the opening game of the World Series in 1971, with Pittsburgh playing Baltimore—the first World Series game, incidentally, that was ever played at night. Her voice isn't a dark mezzo, but a bright, hot mezzo, and she sang beautifully—but in the key of B-flat, which of course took her to the F at the top of the staff—and barely anyone joined in. Not that I minded—I could listen to her all night. But—hardly anyone joined in.

There also pops into my mind, in this connection, my mother, who was also an eminent singer—not quite as eminent as Miss Miller, but quite eminent, at that. She would always make it a point to attend the Washington's Birthday exercises my father elected himself to take charge of. He was president of Washington College, at Chestertown, on the Eastern Shore, which was named for George Washington, and as Washington was one of the college's founders, having kicked in a hundred pounds toward its endowment, my father thought his birthday rated special treatment. The program, as arranged by him, called for the Star-Spangled Banner, under the leadership of the student choir, at that time, of course, in the key of C, which took things to G above the staff. But by a funny coincidence, when choir, students, and even my father had quit from sheer throat collapse, there was my mother and her incomparable voice, perched on the G, with a beautiful bell-like tone and no hint of collapse at all. I used to assume that she went over to the exercises out of respect for George Washington, but now I begin to wonder. Was it that, or perhaps the chance to hog this spot, the opportunity it gave her, to bang out that high note for all and sundry to hear?

Glancing down at the newspaper article that started me off on this piece, I see a reproduction of Schirmer's latest publication of the Star-Spangled Banner, in A-flat. I congratulate Schirmer on waking up, at long last, to the key that people can sing in.

The Star-Spangled Banner is singable, now that at last we let it be.

*Washington Post*
July 3, 1977

# To Keep A Mocking Bird

As I begin to write it is early summer, and for a month I have been an object of curiosity to passers-by in their cars, as I stand in front of my house, here in University Park, Maryland, every morning, my mouth hanging open, my head tilted back, my eyes staring up toward the sky. To my neighbors, however, I am a comprehensible spectacle, for they all know what I am doing there, and what impels me to make such a show of myself.

Well, there's no mystery about it. I am simply drinking in the most beautiful music the morning knows, and trying to locate its source. That isn't always so easy as the music's source is a bird, a mockingbird to be exact, but where he sits while giving his moving serenade is not always so easy to see. However, by moving sidewise, up and down the street, squinting and lining things up in the foliage, I can usually spot him. He's been up there now for a month, having come late this year, perhaps on account of the cold winter we've just had—but his song goes on and on.

To my ear, of all the bird songs I've heard, it is incomparably the most beautiful, differing from other bird songs in that it goes on and on continuously, not merely as a repetition of some brief chirp, trill, or warble. If it is a compendium of other bird calls, strung together so it mocks their calls as legend has it, I don't know. It's hard to be sure about such things, but to my ear it is a succession of endlessly liquid figures, which he persists in once he spots me down there listening—as he seems to do, before really giving out for my benefit.

I can't say the neighborhood pays much attention to him or even to me. But he has his own way of seeking attention—and when he seeks attention he gets it. There are, for example, the Kisielnicki cars which stand in their drive just across from my back yard. Their drive is a double one that they share with the people who live next door to them, and what their car has to do with the mockingbird I had no idea, until Thelma Kisielnicki explained it. It seems that she was out there, about to drive off on an errand, when she discovered she couldn't, on account of the condition of her car. On its side, behind the rear-vision mirror, was our friend the mockingbird, in a dither of rage at the bird he saw in the glass. But birds will be birds, and of course the car, in front of the mirror, was a mess with droppings, so Thelma had to hose the car off, then give it a rub with swatches of dampened papers.

But even that wasn't quite the end of the story. For Thelma had no sooner cleaned things up than the bird shifted its position to the other side of the mirror, so it could really get through and settle the hash of this insolent interloper it knew had to be there. So Thelma had to start with her hose and paper all over again. So then, as one way of dealing with the situation, she and the other Kisielnickis whose cars were parked in the drive, put paper bags on their mirrors, which took care of the situation, but certainly gave them an odd look.

But the next day when Thelma, knowing my interest in the bird, told me about it, I said: "You'll now think me a bit off on the subject, but I could swear I heard him last night—that same pestiferous bird, singing, out there in the dark."

"Not in the dark," she corrected me. "Yes, you're right, he stays out there, under the street lamp, and keeps right on with his serenade." Then, having lived in California, I told how the bird sings through the night out there, leading me to wonder if it and the nightingale of much more poetic fame, aren't really the same bird. It so happened I had heard a nightingale on the superb record Respighi used in his suite "The Pines of Rome," and wrote an orchestral accompaniment for. "It is an overwhelming thing," I told Thelma, she not having heard it, "but so similar to our friend out there in the night—who is also, leave us face it—overwhelming. I honestly can hardly tell the difference."

Well, short of catching a nightingale, bringing him here to the U.S.A., setting him alongside our friend who lives by her drive, having a look at which bird is which—or in some way getting thorough about it, I know of no way to be sure. I know one thing, though: Friend Nightingale might be in some danger, for our bird takes on all comers, in mirrors or wherever one suddenly pops up—as Thelma found out in a somewhat unexpected way. By the end of a few weeks she had spotted our visitor's nest, in a clump of bushes between her back yard and the back yard of her neighbor, close to the ground, as seems to be his habit. But suddenly, toppling out, fell a mockingbird chick, fat, feathery, and more or less helpless as it flopped around in the grass.

So comes it then the cat that lives up the street—a black one, trotting along, belly close to the ground, in a way that meant business—and soon. Do you think that fazed our mockingbird? If so, he hasn't revealed himself unto you, by means of these fragmentary observations. That cat got the surprise of his life. The bird started bombing him. He flew over, hovering, then dived down for the cat's eyes, scoring time and again. Then, almost at once, the cat knew he had had enough, and scutted off to where he lives up the street. Thelma, who had been concerned, breathed easier, and decided that where a mockingbird is concerned, things will come out all right if he's just left alone for a while.

Well, I still lie awake at night, watching the patch of light on the wall, and listening to that music outside, and still puzzle passersby, as I stand enchanted in front of my house. So, I guess that ends my tale, pointless except for the observation that singers are big in the chest, and it's best not to shove them around—or try to.

But if they can sing, that's what we came for, isn't it?

*The Washington Post*
August 14, 1977

# Is A Coluratura

"*A*re *you insinuating that my daughter is a snake?*"

"*No—is a coluratura soprano, is much worse. A little snake, love mamma, do what papa tells, maybe, but a coloratura soprano, love nobody but own goddam self. Is son-bitch-bast', worse than all a snake in a world. Madame, you leave dees girl alone.*"

As Mildren sat blinking, trying to get adjusted to the wholly unexpected turn the interview had taken, Mr. Treviso took another turn around the room, then apparently became more interested in his subject than he had intended. He sat down now, his eyes shining with that Latin glare that had so upset her on her first visit. Tapping her knee again, he said: "*Dees girl, she is coluratura, inside, outside, all over.*"

"*What* is *a coluratura soprano?*"

"*Madame, is special fancy breed, like blue Persian cat. Come once in a lifetime, sing all a trill, a staccato ha-ha-ha, cadenza, a tough stuff—*"

"*Oh, now I understand.*"

"*Cost like 'ell. If is* real *coloratura, bring more dough to a grand opera house than big wop tenor. And dees girl, is coloratura, even a bones is coloratura. First, must know all a rich pipple. No rich, no good.*"

"*She always associated with nice people.*"

"*Nice maybe, but must be rich. All coloratura, they got, 'ow you say?—da gimmies. Always take, never give. O.K., you spend plenty money on dees girl, what she do for you?*"

"*She's a mere child. She can't be expected to—*"

"*So—she do nothing for you. Look.*"

Mr. Treviso tapped Mildred's knee again, grinned. "*She even twiddle la valiere all a coloratura, sit back like a duchess twiddle a la valiere.*" And he gave a startling imitation of Veda, sitting haughtily erect in her chir, twiddling the ornament of her neck chain.

"*She's done that since she was a little girl!*"

"*Yes—is a funny part.*"

Warming up now, Mr. Treviso went on: "*All a coloratura crazy for rich pipple, all take no give, all act like a duchess, all twiddle a la valiere, all a same, every one. All borrow ten t'ousand bucks, go to Italy, study voice, never pay back a money, t'ink was all friendship.*"

*Sing in grand opera, marry a banker, get da money. Got da money, kick out a banker, marry a baron, get da title. 'Ave a sweetie on a side, guy she like to sleep wit'. Den all travel together, all over Europe, grand opera to grand opera, 'otel—a baron, 'e travel in Compartment C, take care of dog. A banker, 'e travel in Compartment B, take care of luggage. A sweetie, 'e travel in Drawing Room A, take care of coloratura—all one big 'appy family. Den come a decoration from King of Belgium—first a command performance, Theatre de la Monnaie, den a decoration. All coloratura 'ave decoration from King of Belgium—first a command performance, Theatre de la Monnaie, den a decoration. All coloratura 'ave decoration from King of Belgium, rest of a life twiddle a la valiere, talk about decoration."*

*"Well—Los Angeles is some distance from Belgium—"*

*"No, no distance. Dees girl, make you no mistake, is big stuff. You know what make a singer? Is first voice, second voice, t'ird voice— yes, all know dees gag. Was Rossini's gag, but maybe even Rossini could be wrong. Must 'ave voice, yes. But is not what make a singer. Must 'ave music, music inside. Caruso, 'e could no read one note, but 'e have music in a soul is come out ever' note 'e sing. Must have rhythm, feel a beat of a music before conductor raise a stick. And specially coloratura—wit'out rhythm, wit'out music, all dees ha-ha-ha is vocalize, not'ing more. O.K., dees Veeda. I work on dees girl one week. She sing full chest, sound very bad, sound like a man. I change to head tone, sound good, I t'ink, yes, 'ere is a voice. 'Ere is one voice in a million. Den I talk. I talk music, music, music. I tell where she go to learn a sight-read, where learn 'armonia, where learn piano. She laugh, say maybe I 'ave somet'ing she can read by sight. On piano is a Stabat Mater, is 'ard, is tricky, is Rossini, is come in on a second beat, sing against accompaniment t'row a singer all off. I say O.K., 'ere is little t'ing you can read by sight. So I begin to play Inflammatus, from a Rossini Stabat Mater. Madame, dees girl hit a G on a nose, read a whole Inflammatus by sight, step into a C like was not'ing at all—don't miss one note. I jump up, I say Jesus Christus, where you come from? She laugh like 'ell. Ask is little 'armonia I want done maybe. Den tell about Charl', and I rememeber her now. Madame, I spend two hours wit' dees girl dees afternoon, and find out she know more music than I know. Den I really look dees girl over. I see dees deep chest, dees big bosom, dees 'igh nose, dees big antrim sinus in front of a face. Den I know what I see. I see what come once in a*

*lifetime only—a great coloratura. I go to work. I give one lesson a day, charge one a week. I bring dees girl along fast, fast. She learn in six mont' what most singer learn in five year, seven year. Fast, fast, fast. I remember Malibran, was artist at fifteen. I remember Melba, was artist at sixteen. Dees girl, was born wit' a music in a soul, can go fast as I take. O.K., you 'ear Snack-O-Ham program?"*

*"Yes, I did."*

*"A Polonaise from Mignon, is tough. She sing like Tetrazzini. Oh, no, Madame, is not far from Los Angeles to Belgium for dees girl. Is no good singer. Is great singer. O.K., ask a pipple. Ask a pipple tuned in on a Snack-O-Ham."*

*Mildred, who had listened to this eulogy as one might listen to soul-nourishing organ music, came to herself with a start and murmured: "She's a wonderful girl."*

*"No—is a wonderful singer."*

*As she looked at him, hurt and puzzled, Mr. Treviso stepped nearer, to make his meaning clear. "Da girl is lousy. She is a bitch. Da singer—is not."*

from *Mildred Pierce*

# III

# PHYSICAL FITNESS
## AND HEALTH

# I N T R O D U C T I O N

□□□□□□□□□□□□□□□□□□□□□□□□

 o the best of my knowledge, the only time James M. Cain ever made an effort to maintain his physical fitness was in 1934, when he invited a friend to go for a long walk with him. This effort to get some exercise was unsuccessful, as the following essay, "Hayfoot, Strawfoot," suggests. He did, however, quit smoking and drinking (which he discusses here in a section from his unpublished memoirs) and it should be noted that although he suffered a heart attack in 1968, he lived to the ripe old age of 85 and was, to the end, mentally alert, and until his last couple of years, quite active physically.

# PHYSICAL FITNESS AND HEALTH

□□□□□□□□□□□□□□□□□□□□□□□□

## Exercise

Putting on clothes, our hero leaves examination room, goes to consultation room, sits down, watches doctor studying card. Gets funny feeling as doctor starts to speak, finds out trouble is pretty serious. Hears long lecture on functions of body, how you can't mistreat it and expect it to give good service, how even machine is entitled to oil, gas, and good handling. "Isn't it?" Agrees that even machine is entitled to oil, gas, and good handling. Hears more, loses place, get back on track again when doctor begins to talk about exercise. Is relieved to find it is as simple as that. Enters into discussion with doctor of various kinds of exercise, rejects golf, handball, tennis and walking because he doesn't like them. Pricks up his ears when doctor says something about skating. Remembers he used to be pretty hot, warms up to idea, admires doctor for insight into muscular play called for by figure 8s, grapevine and speed skating. Stays long time, finally makes up mind skating is just what he needs to fix him up.

Starts home, decides to keep plan secret from wife, so he can practice up and surprise her some time, gets home, tells wife all about it at once. Gets sore when she says it sounds like a nut idea to her. Says that's because she doesn't understand skating. Says she might be interested to know he used to be a skater, and a pretty good one, if he does say it himself. Is glad when she changes the subject, decides his big mistake was to say anything about it at all. Next day tells her he will be home a little late, goes to Spalding's in lunch hour, spends $34 for cap, stockings, sweater and skates screwed on shoes, takes them to office. Sees surprise on secretary's face, decides best thing would be to take her into confidence, does so. Leaves early for Iceland. On subway, notices pretty girl carrying skates, smiles at her, feels pretty proud when she smiles back. Gets off with her, says "Well, I guess we're headed for same place," hears her say, "Yes, I guess so." Carries her skates for her, leaves her at door, gets promise she will skate with him. Goes down, rents locker for months, puts on skates, stockings, cap and sweater, mumbles to self, "How long has this been going on?" Mumbles to self, "I'll say I'm all for skating. Sure, it's a swell form of exercise." Takes look in mirror. Tilts cap to one side. Clumps upstairs.

Starts for rink, hears somebody say "Hello," turns around, sees it is wife. Gets queer feeling in pit of stomach. Says, "Well, what are you doing here?" Hears her say, "Never mind. A little bird told me you were going to be here. I thought I better come up and carry home the pieces." Says, "You won't have any pieces to carry home, ha ha ha." Out of tail of eye, sees girl sail out on ice. Does not look at her. Lights cigaret. Starts mumbling talk about how swell skating is for the leg muscles, how much better it is when they have music. Hears wife say, "Sure, it's good for the leg muscles, but why don't you skate? I want to see some of this fancy stuff." Says, "I will, don't worry, soon as I finish this cigaret." Sees girl coming around, tries to walk to corner, finds skates greatly impede movement, feels girl pluck sleeve as she slides by, hears her cry. "Here I am."

Fishes for Murad, doesn't find any, hears wife say, "Who is she?" Says, "Aw, just a girl I met on the way up." Hears wife say, "She seems to expect you. You better not keep her waiting." Says, "No, she doesn't expect me." Hears wife say, "I think she does." Feels sick, looks at wife, sees queer look on her face, begins to get angry. Says "Well, maybe she does expect me. What of it?" Hears wife say "Nothing. I would go out to her if I were you." Says, "All right, I will." Sees girl coming around again, starts out on ice, motions to girl, has feeling of suspended animation as she takes hold of hand. Spins as she pulls him, sees skate flashing in front of him, hits ice resounding blow, hears boy yell "Set 'em up in the next alley!"

Picks self up, locates girl, takes her hand, tries to skate, can't.

Hears girl say, "Come on, strike out this way, use both your feet, you can't get along using only one." Nods head, says "Sure, I know." Strikes out with both feet, finds one going east, other going north, gets them together with great effort, sits down abruptly on ice. Hears boy bawl, "Safe at second." Gets up, hears girl say, "You must have been roller skating lately. Look, in roller skating you put your weight on your heels. See?" Tries to put weight on heels, begins to fall backward, takes step, goes into dizzy can-can, reels, staggers, hits ice terrible blow, hears shriek, turns head, discovers he has landed at feet of wife.

Says to girl, "You go on. I guess I've kind of forgot how." Hears girl say, "Oh, it'll come back to you," sees her dash away with obvious relief. Picks self up, clumps to bench, sits down beside wife, sees her wipe eyes and try to control hysterics. Says, "Well, what's so damn funny about it?" Says, "Well, if you hadn't skated for twenty years I guess you'd be a little out of practice too." Says, "All right, laugh. What are you doing up here anyway?" Decides secretary must have let cat out of bag. Decides to fire secretary. Says, "All right, you've laughed enough now, come on, we're going home." Decides it is last time for him.

*New York World* column
February 15, 1931

# Hayfoot, Strawfoot

Mr. Charles Hanson Towne, writing of walking on this page, got me so steamed up on that pastime that I decided to try it. I proceeded exactly as he said. I rigged myself out in comfortable clothes. I provided myself with a stick, a good stout shillalah that had stood in the closet a long time, and was thoroughly seasoned.

I invited a male, not a female, companion. We started out, and it was a dreadful flop. We got in a fair amount of talk but not as much talk as we would have got in if we had stayed home by the fire. We covered a fair amount of ground, but not as much ground as we would have covered if we had used a car. Something was the matter, and at the end of five miles we stopped, looked at each other, and went to have a glass of beer and consider what was to be done. There we were offered a ride home, and took it.

On the way back we talked it over, and decided that what ailed it was that we had nothing to look at. "It's like a slow train through Arkansas," said the gentleman who gave us the lift. "All the same, no matter which way you go, so you might just as well sit down on a fire hydrant and take a load off your feet." That summed it up, I think, very neatly. If we had struck for the open road we should have had our coattails fanned by passing cars every ten seconds, and been nervous about getting killed. When we elected to stick to sidewalks, all we saw was usual-looking streets, with houses on them, exactly like the one we started from.

That, no doubt, is why throughout most of the United States walking has fallen into a decline; why nobody walks, if he can help it, and why even those who do walk don't like it much.

In New York I used to walk, quite a lot. I had a friend who like to walk, and as he lived in upper Park avenue and I near Gramercy Park, we could walk either to his place or mine, after having dinner in the forties, and there would be plenty to look at along the way. Every five minutes brought us into a different neighborhood, with different shops, different smells, different people. It was like walking in Europe—the scale was so small, the life so varied, that you had a sense of change, of having got somewhere, with very little effort.

But outside the cities, this country is too vast to give you that without an expenditure of time and labor out of all proportion to what it is worth. From where I live, for example, I can reach snow-covered mountains, or the sea, or the California orange country with an hour's drive. But to reach any of them afoot means a whole day of plodding. I can't give a whole day to walking. Two hours is what I figure on, but two hours, in these great spaces, take me nowhere.

The shoe manufacturers, I think, ought to go into this subject, for it concerns them. I have four pairs of shoes—two blacks, one tan, the other a vague chocolate color. All were bought in New York, before I left for California two years ago. Not one of them shows the slightest sign of wear, not one of them has even had a new pair of rubber heels tacked on. From that you can get a rough idea how little exercise I take.

I think the shoe business ought to get behind the slogan: *Wear Out Your Shoes and Stay Young*.

Hearst column
February 28, 1934

# Doctors and Cooking

For all we know to the contrary, this decision on the part of Johns Hopkins Medical School to teach their students cookery during their final year may be admirable, if regarded purely from a professional point of view. That is to say, since diet has come to play such an important part in the treatment of diseases, this course may actually make the students better doctors. Nevertheless, we view it with considerable misgiving. For obviously it is only another indication of a tendency that has become all too noticeable in the last few years, and that is the tendency to make caloric correctitude the criterion of cookery, instead of taste. There was a time when this was not the case, and you could go into an American restaurant and get a meal that was a pleasure to eat. But now eating for pleasure has gone out of fashion. Dietetics rule the day, and there is hardly a hotel that does not offer its miserable vegetable plate, its glass of specially treated milk or its patent stewed figs, and hardly a man to lunch with who does not babble of his proteids, his carbohydrates and his vitamins—until the art of eating has become indistinguishable from the art of getting your appendix cut out.

Somehow this strikes us as very dubious, not only as hedonism, but also as hygiene, which is supposed to be its forte. Is there any real virtue, after all, in tastelessness? Is a boiled potato any better for you than potato au gratin? Is there any real harm in a filet mignon with mushrooms? Is there anything about that dreadful blend, carrots and peas, to compensate for its horrible taste? We have our doubts. As a rule, it seems to us that what tastes good, if you use any judgement at all, is likely to agree with you, and that munching down what does not taste good, simply for its supposed dietetic value, is useless suffering. Also, it is very dangerous to provide cooks with an alibi. It used to be that if the dish was improperly prepared you could send it back and there would be no questions asked. Now the waiter tells you that this particular style is recommended by all the best doctors, no doubt graduates of the Johns Hopkins Medical School. What this country needs, in our opinion, is fewer dieticians and more cooks.

*New York World* editorial
September 5, 1928

# No Proteids

Some years ago, when I served a short term in a tuberculosis sanatorium, the superintendent addressed me thus: "Now, you've got tuberculosis. You haven't got it bad, and if you're careful you can live to a ripe old age, have plenty of fun, and do plenty of work. But you've got it, and all your friends, and the whole world that you live in, have got to know you've got it. If they do, they'll be considerate of you, and not expect you to play tennis, or crank a stalled car, or do any of the things that will send you off the deep end. But if they don't, if you try to hide it, you're headed for trouble, because sooner or later you'll play that tennis game, or crank that car, and it's curtains for you. Now remember what I'm telling you. They die of this disease. If you want to beat that rap, you do it the way I say, and hang a sign on yourself, and then maybe they'll let you live."

I did it the way he said, and it worked the way he said. But then a complication arose. Lung trouble is usually followed by liver trouble. For one thing, the lung involvement has an organic effect on the liver, and for another thing, the forced feeding which a lung involvement calls for, the endless eggs and milk that you have to consume to bring your weight up, puts a strain on your liver and it cracks up.

When that happened with me, that is right where my trouble started. For some reason I don't mind the confession about the lung. As a matter of fact, you don't have to say anything about it very often, and even then people don't pound the subject much. But this liver thing is an old man of the sea wherever I go. You see, with a weak liver you don't dare drink. That means that when I am invited out I have to decline the cocktail. Common courtesy demands some sort of mumbled explanation, but this usually provokes a sales talk from the host. Partly he wants to be hospitable, and partly he begins to be worried when he finds a teetotaler in the room, for sad experience has taught him that teetotalers make bad parties. Then comes a fuller explanation, and if it comes out that I am permitted a little wine now and then, there follows the dive for the sherry bottle, and I begin to feel like a nuisance. And by that time the whole room is discussing my liver, and Uncle Charlie's liver, and Grandpop's diabetes, and an exceedingly dull subject is definitely on the agenda for at least a half hour, and I wish I had never brought it up.

The same thing is repeated at dinner when it is noticed that I am going easy on the meat. There is usually the proffer of an omelette at this point, but then I have to explain that eggs are even a worse poison to me than meat is, or liquor. And so, we are off again.

What I am trying to say is that the person on a diet has a much worse time of it than anybody realizes. People think he faces an eating problem, but what he really faces is a social problem. And, of course, every so often he weakens, and takes the cocktail, and eats the meat, and then next morning, and for a whole week thereafter, pays the dreadful, aching penalty.

What do you do in a case like this? I have never figured out anything to do. It is either talk about it or seem rude, but I am getting to the point where I think seeming rude is the more humane course. I am seriously thinking of clearing the whole thing up by claiming to be a cousin to Mr. Andy Volstead.

Hearst column
February 20, 1934

# On Giving Up Drinking and Smoking

*(In 1942, Cain had an operation called a Finney pylorectomy, which he commented on in his unpublished memoirs)*

I found out something after my operation I could better have gone on not knowing. I could drink now without a hangover. The reason was that the Finney pylorectomy they did on me cut out the pylorus, or acid-forming part of my stomach—the rest being sutured to the duodenum, the short connecting link between stomach and small gut (as doctors always call it—they never say "intestine"—which is also where all stomach digestive juices empty, especially bile and pancreatic fluid.) Well, in my stomach was left no tissue to secrete acid, meaning I could drink all I wanted with impunity—and did. Alas, alas, and alas, I did. My face began to have that beet-red undertone that comes out of only one pot. I didn't become a problem drinker—I didn't lie down in the gutter, or argue loudly, or sing, or become a problem—not much of a problem anyway. It went on and on and on, for the rest of the time I stayed in Los Angeles, until Florence, my little opera-singer wife that I married in middle age, began to get concerned. Very sagacious, she knew the one thing not to do with a drunk is begin hacking at him to get him to stop. But her concern went on and on, until after we moved to Maryland.

And then one night I wanted to tell her a funny story about John Charles Thomas, whom she had sung with, and his singing of *Di Provenza Il Mar*, the big baritone aria at a Metropolitan broadcast of Traviata. When Mostyn Thomas, a San Carlos baritone, rang me to know if I'd heard it, and to rave at how terrific it was, I broke in: "But Mostyn, didn't he sing the last verse first?" "Yes, of course!" he answered. "He's been doing it for years. Somebody's going to tell him one of these days."

So when I started to tell her about it, I opened my mouth to refresh her recollection of how the second verse went—and the words didn't come. Now something you learned at the age of nineteen is part of you, and not being able to remember it means something. I finished my tale without singing any words, and shortly after that came down with the flu—so for some days I carried a fever. With a fever you can't drink, and of course I didn't. At the end of a week when I stood in front of the mirror to shave off this weird-looking white fuzz all over my face, I remembered *Traviata*. And at once the second verse of *Di Provenza* came: I knew then I had to stop drinking.

It was a most terrible, frightening realization. It kept torturing me. And then suddenly I thought of my little cousin Ruth White, Ruth Clifford later on, and the visit she paid us in Annapolis at the age of eight, she having learned a show-off piece on the piano, that let her cross one hand over the other, a piece that also had words:

> On a summer day,
> Sing a merry lay,
> Bobolink, bobolink
> Spink, spank, spink
> Bobolink, bobolink,
> Spink, spank, spink
And I thought:
> Bobolink, boblink,
> Spink, spank, spink

All a drunk wants
Is one more drink.
Not four,
Not three,
Not two
Just one!

I thought to myself, well that's a help.

I thought of the old principle, believed by most people, and certainly by me: an alcoholic is never more than one drink from disaster. After a long time, many weeks, I came up as though I was Einstein discovering the Theory of Relativity, with:

And never more than one drink from salvation.

I lived with that for some time before I thought: "Well, instead of that forever-and-a-day that seems to demoralize you so, how about skipping that one drink? Then, if you slip, nothing much has happened to cut your throat about. But then, if you don't slip, you've skipped that one drink."

Florence didn't drink much, but she wouldn't let me drink alone, and after dozens of evenings when I didn't skip anything, she reached one evening for the orange to begin making our Old-Fashioneds, but I heard myself say: "Can't we postpone on that?" And she, staring, said, "Oh, all right." After dinner, she asked: "Well? the usual?"

And I answered: "I think I'll pass it up."

"All right," she said.

So, that evening, I skipped two Old Fashioneds and two "Pink Drinks," as we called the Dubonnet and gin I had ordinarily finished the day with. So? Only four drinks had made me a drunk? That's right, but I had had those four every night.

From there on in, she didn't mention drink—and I didn't. The subject simply didn't come up. But then, after a couple of years it did come up, and she said: "Well, I knew of course what you had to be going through, and was all ready with warm, encouraging remarks to help you bear it. But you never said one word. I began to wonder then if I knew you as well as I thought I did."

On this subject of swearing off this and that, there's a little more, leading to a big decision. The cooling-off process of my stomach, it turned out, was to give it a chance to regain its normal condition, instead of being all swelled up "like a sore lip," as Bob Rathbone put it. And then one day in his office the doctor began to talk about smoking. "I never order a patient to stop smoking," he said. "I explain what smoking does to him, and leave it to his judgement." As he said that I squashed a cigarette out in his ash tray, the smallest, meanest little ash tray I ever saw, and as I did I said to myself: "If you have any brains, that will be your last one."

I went home, I had dinner, still with no cigarette, and then sweeping over me came this compulsion "what I wouldn't give for a smoke." I said to myself, "Knock it off—you've smoked your last cigarette." So it turned out, and on the flat decision I made, the deprivation vanished. I can't say it was easy, but by bedtime I knew I had quit.

At this point, I think a few observations by me, about smoking and drinking, on the basis of my kicking both, might be helpful to those up against the same problem I was up against. To begin with, the drinking problem is always discussed in terms of "alcoholism," as though some of us become alcoholics. But this misses the whole point.

So, while I'm on this subject I've dealt with successfully, first-hand, let me make a few observations, telling the little I know about it.

In the first place, about drinking, most that is said about it sets up a false distinction involving what are usually called "alcoholics." The person who can't stop after the second cocktail, or the one whose speech begins to thicken after one cocktail, are called by their friends "alcoholics," as though this explains them, and they are somehow exceptional. This I dispute. It is true as far as it goes, but it doesn't go far enough. It ignores the indisputable factor that actually we are all alcoholics—and not only we, but all other warm-blooded things created by God. Cattle, when they come on the refuse pile of mash from some mountain still, gobble it down and then run around bellowing, before stretching out on the ground and bringing it up as cud. My little cat, when children brought him to the door on Christmas Day, lapped up the eggnog I poured him, then began staggering around, daring me to fight. We are all alcoholics—those of us who are not, who don't like drinks with alcohol in them, are so exceptional as to have no real effect on the rule.

So, what to do about it? In my belief, the only thing that meets the issue involves that ugly little four-letter word STOP.

Yes, but how?

Alcoholics Anonymous, which hadn't come along at the time I decided to stop, knows how, and I can't commend them too strongly. They start with the idea that misery loves company—but this gnawing, incessant, special kind of misery needs very special company, and Alcoholics Anonymous provides it—provides the chance to talk about it with that God-given companion, somebody else in the same box. I didn't talk about it—I stopped cold turkey, saying nothing about it to anyone. But that was because I had no one to talk to, and the only person who can help, in this case, is somebody else in the same box. So, let's take off our hat to Alcoholics Anonymous, an outfit that does a very great work and does it very well.

Still, when all that has been said, there comes that certain point involving that same old word, STOP. In other words, to reach the heaven of peace, when the desire for drink doesn't come any more, in one way or another way, we have to endure one other four-letter word, a little bit of HELL.

It's hell all right. Don't kid yourself, it is. But, if you'll only be brave, hell won't last forever, and when you're done with it you're done, if you'll only let yourself be, meaning, if you only let it alone, keep what you've won, and begin to live again. I don't think you can half stop, "cut down," use it in "moderation," as they say. You have to go off it altogether, but when you do manage to go off it, when you're out from under, you'll have entered a new phase. Once more, life will be worth living.

But now, as I leave the subject of alcohol and move on to tobacco, I have to say backwards everything I've been saying—for nobody, let me repeat nobody, is born with a taste for tobacco. And the psychological riddle is, why should anyone go through the agony, the nausea, the dizziness, the utter misery, of that first cigarette, that second cigarette, the third, the fourth, the tenth—for it takes that long to "learn to smoke," to acquire the habit, in other words, so to smoke becomes a necessity, an insistent, nagging compulsion.

In my belief, the psychological basis of it is histrionic. That is, in the beginning, and to some extent as a continuing factor, I think we smoke partly for the picture the cigarette, and other forms of tobacco, give us of ourselves. With that cigarette between our fingers, we imagine ourselves devilishly careless, debonair. Of course, others may not see us that way, but how we see ourselves is the main thing, at this point. With a cigar, we imagine ourselves important, well-heeled, rich—or the appearance of rich. With a pipe we are deep, intelligent, and profound. With a calabash we are a bit like Sherlock Holmes— reflective, observant, English. Nevertheless, whatever the original psychological basis of this habit, its physical effect, its compulsive drag on the lungs, its demanding need, once acquired goes a way beyond psychology, and becomes a physical thing, a hunger for what in all essential respects is a drug. And to break out becomes a necessity. Well, how? On this problem I have little to offer, I'm afraid, that is going to help—little, that is, that is going to make stopping easier. For the time will come when you must STOP. The penalties for not stopping, of course, are horrendous—cancer of the throat, of the lung, of course, are among them. Still, as one who has been through the mill, let me assure you: the second when you do put yourself through the wringer, is worth it. You are free of this dreadful habit, this thing that gives you no peace, that merely leads to this cigarette after that last cigarette. You can quit if you mean to quit. It will mean a bad three days, perhaps one bad half-hour at the end of a month. But that is all, in most cases. At the end of six months you are done with it—and it is done with you.

Lecture one. If you decide to stop I'll pray for you, and wish you luck.

# IV

# ANIMALS

*S*he was a light-haired girl, maybe a little older than I was, and not bad on looks. But what got me was how friendly she was, and how she wasn't any more afraid of what I might do to her than if I was a kid or something. She knew her way around all right, you could see that. And what finished it was when I found out she didn't know who I was. We told our names on the way out, and to her mine didn't mean a thing. Boy oh boy what a relief that was. One person in the world that wasn't asking me to sit down to the table a minute, and then telling me to give them the low-down on that case where they said the Greek was murdered. I looked at her, and I felt the same way I had walking away from the train, like I was made of gas, and would float out from behind the wheel.

"So your name is Madge Allen, hey?"

"Well, it's really Kramer, but I took my own name again after my husband died."

"Well listen Madge Allen, or Kramer, or whatever you want to call it, I've got a little proposition to make you."

"Yes?"

"What do you say we turn this thing around, point her south, and you and me take a little trip for about a week?"

"Oh, I couldn't do that?"

"Why not?"

"Oh, I just couldn't, that's all."

"You like me?"

"Sure I like you."

"Well, I like you. What's stopping us?"

She started to say something, didn't say it, and then laughed. "I own up. I'd like to, all right. And if it's some-

*thing I'm supposed not to do, why that don't mean a thing
to me. But I can't. It's on account of the cats."*

*"Cats?"*

*"We've got a lot of cats. And I'm the one that takes
care of them. That's why I had to get home."*

*"Well, they got pet farms, haven't they? We'll call one
up, and tell them to come over and get them."*

*That struck her funny. "I'd like to see a pet farm's face
when it saw them. They're not that kind."*

*"Cats are cats, ain't they?"*

*"Not exactly. Some are big and some are little. Mine
are big. I don't think a pet farm would do very well with
that lion we've got. Or the tigers. Or the puma. Or the
three jaguars. They're the worst. A jaguar is an awful cat."*

*"Holy smoke. What do you do with those things?"*

*"Oh, work them in movies. Sell the cubs. People have
private zoos. Keep them around. They draw trade."*

*"They wouldn't draw my trade."*

*"We've got a restaurant. People look at them."*

*"Restaurant, hey. That's what I've got. Whole goddam
country lives selling hot dogs to each other."*

*"Well, anyway, I couldn't walk out on my cats. They've
got to eat."*

*"The hell we can't. We'll call up Goebel and tell him
to come get them. He'll board the whole bunch while we're
gone for a hundred bucks."*

*"Is it worth a hundred bucks to you to take a trip with
me?"*

*"It's worth exactly a hundred bucks."*

*"Oh my. I can't say no to that. I guess you better call
up Goebel."*

*I dropped her off at her place, found a pay station,
called up Goebel, went back home, and closed up. Then I
went back after her. It was about dark. Goebel had sent a
truck over, and I met it coming back, full of stripes and
spots. I parked about a hundred yards down the road, and
in a minute she showed up with a little grip, and I helped
her in, and we started off.*

*"You like it?"*

*"I love it."*

We went down to Caliente, and next day we kept on down the line to Ensenada, a little Mexican town about seventy miles down the coast. We went to a little hotel there, and spent three or four days. It was pretty nice. Ensenada is all Mex, and you feel like you left the U.S.A. a million miles away. Our room had a little balcony in front of it, and in the afternoon we would just lay out there, look at the sea, and let the time go by.

"Cats, hey. What do you do, train them?"

"Not the stuff we've got. They're no good. All but the tigers are outlaws. But I do train them."

"You like it?"

"Not much, the real big ones. But I like pumas. I'm going to get an act together with them some time. But I'll need a lot of them. Jungle pumas. Not these outlaws you see in the zoos."

"What's an outlaw?"

"He'd kill you."

"Wouldn't they all?"

"They might, but an outlaw does anyhow. If it was people, he would be a crazy person. It comes from being bred in captivity. These cats you see, they look like cats, but they're really cat lunatics."

from *The Postman Always Rings Twice*

# INTRODUCTION

□□□□□□□□□□□□□□□□□□□□□□□

ain had a theory about our fascination with animals, which he explained in one of his 1934 syndicated columns:

The other day, driving around one of California's small lakes, we saw many charming things. We saw a bluebird, a catbird, a red-headed woodpecker. We saw wild ducks nibbling at reeds, big frogs squatting on lily pads. We saw a crane, standing in the shallows with one leg tucked up under it. We saw a squirrel, a rabbit bouncing off into the brush, and for one brief glimpse, a deer. And then, erasing all this from our recollections, we saw a spider.

It was so big, and its gait so ungainly, that at first I thought it was a crippled chipmunk, and pulled out to avoid it. Then I saw what it was, with this curious result: I automatically pulled up the brake. All those other things, mind you, we had seen, looked at, commented on, and passed by without so much as slowing down, in spite of the fact that they suggested what we felt was beauty. But, at this horrible apparition, it was instinctive for us to get our of the car, stare fascinated at the great black body, at least two inches long; at the hairy legs, as large as a small lobster's, at the thick mandibles, at the singularly malevolent eyes. Why was this?

Friends, I have a theory that what we call "fascination" is merely the imaginative side of fear. We say a spider fascinates us, or a tiger, or a shark, or a woman, and so they do as long as the situation puts us out of their reach. But let the situation change ever so slightly, let the spider get on our leg, the tiger out of his sage, the shark close to shore, or the woman into our life, and they don't fascinate us any more! They terrify us, and it is the knowledge of the terror inside us that lends the special quality to what we feel as fascination.

I must confess that all derivatives of fear interest me enormously. I am unable to write a story until I have trapped my characters into a spot where fear is the one emotion they react to. I think it is stronger than love, hate, hunger, thirst, grief, and all other emotions added together. But it has its strange, terrible beauties too . . . I'll remember that spider. Maybe I can work it into a story sometime.

To my knowledge, Cain never wrote a story about spiders, but he did write several about the animals that fascinated him most—cats, of all sizes. Early evidence of his own fascination with the big cats came in the 1920s, when he wrote the following editorial for *The New York World*, printed in its entirety:

### QUERY

Apropos of nothing whatever, what *does* one do on meeting a man-eating tiger?

One response came from the American representative of the Indian National Railways, who lived in New York. It was in the form of a 1,200-word letter stating in detail what one actually does on meeting a man-eating tiger, which Cain boiled down to "climb a tree fast, as fast as God will let you and stay there, three days if necessary, until help comes or the tiger goes away, which isn't all that guaranteed."

*The World* printed the letter and it was reprinted in newspapers all across the country. Then came an article from another gentleman arguing that the tiger was a very noble beast, to which Cain responded with this editorial:

Some days ago we published an article by Dudley Nichols which had to do with the tiger. It was an extended interview with a gentleman from India, and the cause of it was that the tiger looks purple in the jungle, instead of black, orange and white as he looks in the Zoo, and that he is a very noble beast. The first of these propositions we are quite prepared to accept. In fact it would not surprise us at all if the tiger when seen in the jungle not only looked purple but also blue, green and tangerine, with a bit of violet thrown in for good measure; how the tiger looks in the jungle must be largely a matter of how fast you can run. But the second proposition, as to the nobility of the tiger's nature, strikes us as very dubious.

We have no deep prejudice against the tiger, mind you; we have an open mind and would be perfectly willing to make friends with him if we had ever heard of a tiger that was in a humor to make friends with anybody. Was any tiger ever in an amiable frame of mind? If so, there is certainly no mention of the fact in the literature of the subject. Mr. Nichol's gentleman from India paints no very reassuring picture. The tiger he describes just before he died, was busy clawing the neck of an elephant. Even Ko-Ko, the Lord High Executioner of the Mikado, who always saw the best in everybody, could say very little for the tiger, for he sang:

Yes, I love to see a tiger

From the Congo or the Niger

And especially when lashing of his tail.

Kipling's tiger, the late-lamented Shere Khan, was a most unmannerly brute, from his first entrance when he stuck his head in the hole and snarled at Mowgli to his demise when Mowgli rang him down with a herd of buffaloes. In fact the only thing we have heard that implies that a tiger might have his tractable moments was a little song that went like this:

Hallelujah, see the tiger!

Hallelujah, hear him purr!

Hallelujah, feed the tiger!

Hallelujah, stroke his fur!

And this, it must be admitted, is hardly calculated to quiet the nerves on the occasion of beholding a purple tiger in the jungle.

To sum up: if any reader can supply us with evidence that the tiger, in spite of his forbidding aspect, really has a heart of gold, we shall be glad to see Grover A. Whalen about giving him the recognition he deserves. But lacking this evidence, we shall continue our present attitude, intelligent scepticism.

When Cain shifted his career from journalism to fiction, he continued his fascination with animals and cats: His first successful California story—"The Baby in the Icebox"—concerned a baby who was put into an icebox to protect him from a big tiger loose in the house. And most of his light fiction centered around animals or mammals. And after *The Magician's Wife* was published in 1965, Cain started to work on a novel about a little girl who discovered too late that the pet she was given to raise was a Siberian Tiger. The story started out easy enough, he wrote one friend, "a little fairy tale I could do with one hand." But then soon it had become a genie he could not get back in the bottle and when he finally finished it and it was rejected by his publisher he was crushed: "I thought a law had been passed that when I wrote a book it sold," he wrote his sister. A few years later, he re-wrote it as a children's book, but it still did not sell.

Cain's own preoccupation with animals was all mixed up with his ideas about God and religion. "I find it impossible to believe in life after death," he wrote one friend, "and if you don't accept that, the Christian theology goes up in smoke . . . To me, God is life, and if no immortal soul figures in, then all must be included in this concept. So animals to me take on a mystic meaning, more perhaps than they do to most people."

When Cain and his fourth wife, Florence, settled in Hyattsville in the 1950s, they owned a little cat called Nickie. As with many childless couples, sometimes in their loneliness their little cat took on special meaning, as Cain suggests in this moving description of one gloomy Christmas in the late 1950s: "We did nothing about it at all except to light our little tree, hold hands and watch the wonder of our little cat, who would creep up on it, stare, and begin to touch the ornaments with his paw. When it would fall down on the rug, he would edge up to it warily, then begin popping it with his paw and then, of course, it would disappear into a little pile of tinsel, and this he couldn't understand. Florence delighted in his bewilderment, felt Christmas to be a birth, a reawakening of all created things, including the animals that gave up their manger, even little cats."

In 1958, Nickie died and they buried him in the Bonheur Memorial Park in Elkridge, Maryland. And Cain wrote the park's manager: "From you, I needn't conceal this was a bereavement that wrenched us both in the deepest part of our nature."

Florence still had "Mr. and Mrs. Cardinal," two little birds. They also bought a new cat, Mittens, and when Florence was confined to her bed with a serious spell of high blood pressure, Cain was certain her life was saved by Mittens, "who stayed with her the whole time and nipped and talked and purred at her, until she began to calm down."

Then Mittens and Florence died, and Cain was writing friends how utterly alone he felt. He acquired a stray cat—Snobby—who wandered into his house on Christmas day, 1969, when Cain was 77 years old. Snobby was sick and Cain planned to send him to an animal hospital but after feeding and nursing him and giving him Kaopectate with an eye-dropper, he could not bear to part with him. So Snobby stayed, and Cain took up a quiet life with his new pet: "I wake up every morning feeling utterly pooped . . . tell myself I owe it to myself to take a day off. I get up, put on my bathrobe, go down in bare feet and let in the cat . . . he is as God created him, without any surgical improvements, and he's going to stay that way if I have anything to do with it. But it means he has to be let out at night, and so around 8 a.m. I go down and let him in. Then for ten minutes we have a snuggle, which he looks forward to and insists on. Then [after feeding Snobby] I read the paper a few minutes. Then I come up, bathe, shave, and dress. Then I go down, finish the paper, broil up my breakfast, and eat it. Then I go to work. After three or four hours of that, I suddenly remember my decision not to work and ask myself what happened to it. I always seem to forget about it. But one of these days, I'll take a day off. In the evening, sometimes people come in—I have a few friends who live nearby and we crack jokes."

One time, Snobby wandered away for five days and returned with a fractured jaw, which Cain had a vet wire. Shortly after that, Cain dozed off for a nap one afternoon with Snobby at his side. When he awoke, Snobby was dead. "Few things in my life have so upset me," he wrote his sister. His relationship with Snobby had been an education he said "and, as always in my relation to other created things, brought me closer to God. The love and devotion that this little creature has shown is an inspiration."

Cain never owned another cat after Snobby, but he did acquire a pet raccoon, which he wrote about in one of his last *Washington Post* articles. And although he described it as the worst organized piece he had ever written, it brought him the most mail he ever received for an article or an editorial or columns written for *The World* and Hearst. James M. Cain had discovered very early what most writers eventually learn—that our fascination with pets and animals is unbounded. And it was an incident concerning an animal that helped him develop one of his own notions about humor. He expounded the theory in this 1934 column for Hearst.

I am not exactly an admirer of Mr. Eugene O'Neill's *Strange Interlude,* or at any rate of the technique he used in telling that tale; and yet there are situations where it is the only thing that fits. For example, there is the situation that developed over Mr. Charles Butterworth, the moving picture actor, and the horse.

Mr. Butterworth had an informal birthday party going on and the guests had brought the usual calico dogs, mechanical snakes and other small gifts deemed appropriate under these circumstances. Then came a ring at the bell, and a brash boy appeared outside, laughing himself double over his gift, which was a live horse, an ancient, bony and decrepit creature, wheezing heavily at the end of a rope. He was tethered to a palm tree outside, and I went out to laugh at him.

Then, as the party was breaking up, Mr. Butterworth said, "This is all very well, but what do I do with this horse now that I've got him?" "Oh, that's all taken care of," said the humorous youth who had brought him. "Gay's Lion Farm is going to call for him in the morning."

So Mr. Butterworth went upstairs and spent the rest of the night looking down at his horse, and shedding pretty salty tears over it. And sure enough, about five o'clock a truck chugged up to the house, and the horse was loaded aboard to be fed to the lions that afternoon.

Now, as one lady observed, you can understand a boy who thought a thing like that was funny, but why did the rest of them laugh at the horse? They weren't peasants, to cackle cruelly at ribs, hips and harness galls: they were civilized people.

My theory is that they laughed because they knew if they didn't laugh the thing would suddenly be so ghastly that it would haunt them for years. That is why I say Mr. O'Neill's technique, which shows the painted grins on their faces and the black thoughts in their hearts, is the only thing that fits in such a case.

What an idea for an evening's pleasantry! What an ordeal to behold it and have to pretend it was funny!

# ANIMALS

□□□□□□□□□□□□□□□□□□□□□□□□

## Fit for a Queen—Worth a King's Ransom

Last winter, being momentarily in funds and wishing to give my wife a fur coat, I strolled into a furrier's on Fifth Avenue, New York. And, having heard my wife express her preference in furs, I told the doorman: "I wish to look at a chinchilla coat."

"Yes sir."

He bowed and disappeared but looked at me so oddly I thought there must be something wrong with my appearance. Checking up furtively in a mirror, I found my apparel in order, and then reflected that after all I probably wasn't this store's type. But when a suave salesman heard my brief announcement, and gave me the same odd stare, I began to wonder what this was about, anyway.

"Well," he said, catching himself quickly, "we don't have a chinchilla coat in stock at the moment: you see there's some little difficulty about getting the skins. But I could show you a chinchilla cape?"

"I had thought about a coat."

"Ah—would you step back?" the salesman inquired. "I could show you the cape, and then perhaps I could find out what could be done about a coat."

So we stepped back, and took seats in an alcove, and presently a model appeared, wearing the cape. I suppose you know what chinchilla looks like: the luminous pearl-gray of the center of the skin; the rich, warm white of the edge, breaking into gray at each movement of the wearer; its depth, beauty and overwhelming voluptuousness. I knew as soon as I set eyes on it that I was looking at one of the great furs of the world. But I no sooner knew this than a certain discomfort began to creep in on me.

For one thing, I began to recall more clearly my wife's remarks on this subject, and the reverence of her words did not exactly harmonize with the sum I had in my pocket. Then it popped into my head about an aunt of mine, an opera singer, and the chinchilla piece she had had, and the commotion this had caused. Then there was that remark of the salesman's about the difficulty of getting skins. Most of all, there was the expression of the model. For all her disarming prettiness, there was a certain coldness in her eye, a look of appraisal when she faced me, that would hardly be called forth by something usual, like mink. In other words, I had a dreadful feeling that when I stuck my foot down I wouldn't touch bottom: that I was away out beyond my depth. However, there was nothing for it but the foot. I turned to the salesman. "And how much is the cape?"

"Twelve thousand dollars."

I drop a time curtain here, to denote a lapse of a painful ten seconds, and pick up at the point where we were all laughing merrily, ha-ha-ha, and I was saying no wonder my wife liked chinchilla, and the salesman was saying as a matter of fact it suited them just as well to keep the cape in stock right now, and the model was saying perhaps there was something *else* I would like to look at. Oh, we were very gay. Even the model was gay. She could afford to be. She *knew* she had my number, all along.

So then we talked about chinchilla in general, and I asked the price of a chinchilla coat, assuming it were possible to get the skins.

"Sixty thousand dollars," said the salesman.

"Bid or asked?"

"Both."

"You mean, if you had a chinchilla coat just now, you could actually find somebody willing to pay you sixty thousand dollars for it?"

"My dear fellow, I could sell it, spot cash at that price, in one minute flat, simply by picking up that telephone."

"What makes it so expensive?"

"Partly the beauty of the fur, partly the demand for it among people able to pay any price for what they want, and partly the scarcity of the skins. The chinchilla is a small Andean animal that has been hunted so much, trapped so much, and protected so little that it is almost extinct. For these reasons, chinchilla has become a fur that makes Russian sable seem cheap. I assure you that this little cape represents our best effort in collecting skins, over a considerable period of time, and that it would be impossible, in New York City today, to assemble a much larger garment."

"It's a wonder that somebody wouldn't have the bright idea of raising these animals in captivity, the way they've done with silver foxes."

"Somebody has had that bright idea. It's being tried, I believe, somewhere out in California, though I don't know with what success."

After this harrowing experience, you may realize that I was rather vividly aware of the chinchilla, and likely, on my return to California, to try and find out more about it. So, in fact, I did. I tracked the chinchilla to the farm, just outside Los Angeles, where it is being raised; I invaded its cabinetmade, scientifically-insulated lair; I made its acquaintance and fell for it even harder than I had fallen for its fur.

It is, I should say, about the size of a squirrel, but on account of the depth of the fur looks considerably bigger, about as big as a small rabbit. Indeed, it looks a little like a squirrel, and a little like a rabbit, and perhaps a little like a woodchuck. And yet it has something that all these animals lack, a personality that is not entirely in the imagination of the beholder, for its comparatively long gestative period of 111 days, the age to which it lives, known to be eighteen years in some cases, and its relatively high intelligence, all mark it as a superior member of the rodent family to which it belongs.

Its head seems large for its body, though here again its thick fur may deceive the eye. Its eyes are large, black and beady. Its ears are shaped like a squirrel's ears, but are considerably larger, with thin edges and delicate veining. Its teeth are small, with four incisors in front and tiny molars behind. The legs are small and their fur very short; the feet have tiny nails, and underneath a small black pad, that feels soft and oily to the touch, like a monkey's paw. The tail is about six inches long, with a curl like a squirrel's, and a bushiness that comes from hairs as wiry as bristles. But the fur is irresistible. It is about an inch and a half deep, as fine as silk, and so thick that a flea smothers in it, one of the reasons a chinchilla is completely free from vermin. The color is pearl-gray on the back, shading off to white on the belly, but a white that has gray underneath it, so that at every movement a hint of gray ripples through, and the fur takes on that animation that is one of its chief characteristics.

It is a gentle little animal, quick to make friends and charmingly inquisitive. But gentleness, of course, is a quality only admirable in the tiger; encountered in a rabbit it doesn't have much point. Thus it is pleasing to learn that the chinchilla has a streak of the tiger in him too. You see he is sometimes visited by snakes, who fix him with their glassy eye, and expect him to sit there, tremble, and wait for death. They get a rude shock. The chinchilla dashes in, bites them once just back of the head, and the snakes die immediately.

Now to explain what it is doing here in California, living a life of pampered ease, I shall have to take you back a few years. As far back as 1919, in fact, when the late M. F. Chapman of Los Angeles was in Potrerillos, Chile, as an engineer for the Anaconda Copper Company. One day an Indian came down from the high peaks with something that was destined, so far as Mr. Chapman was concerned, to be worth more than two or three copper mines. It was a live chinchilla, in a box.

Mr. Chapman knew something of the history of this animal. He knew that in the early 1900's, skins to the number of several hundred thousand had been annually exported, and that chinchilla was one of the important industries of the country. And he knew thay by 1915 the number had dropped to less than 5,000, and that two years later the situation had become so serious that the government prohibited all export, all trapping, and all hunting. But he also knew that these measures weren't likely to do much good. For the real threat to the chinchilla wasn't commerce. It was the red foxes that Englishmen had brought into the country, so they could have their hunting. So when he saw this animal, vague ideas of saving it from extinction began to revolve in his mind, and he bought it.

Then he reflected that he would have to mate it if anything were to come of his ideas, and decided presently to grub-stake some Indians, and offer them more for the live animals than they could possibly get for skins. So he sent two dozen Indians up into the high places, and they trapped for three years. At the end of that time, Mr. Chapman had eleven animals to show for his pains, but fortunately three of them were females.

He then undertook the ticklish job of getting them to the United

States. As he was a person of position, the Chilean government coöperated with the necessary permits for export, but the captain of the Japanese ship was a problem. Just to avoid trouble, Mr. Chapman took one whole deck of the steamer, but that didn't do any good. The captain took a pigs-is-pigs attitude, and decreed that live animals would have to go in the hold. No argument swayed him. So then Mr. Chapman resorted to direct action, for he knew that in the hold these animals would die, as they would have to have ice, air, and perhaps even electric fans to help them carry their fabulous coats of fur across the equatorial heat. He had eleven of his friends put live chinchillas in their pockets and come aboard to say goodbye. He had the cage carried on in the guise of a trunk. When the animals were safely in his stateroom, he served notice on the captain that they were worth $1,000,000 cash; that if anything happened to them he would libel the ship for that amount, and hold it in San Pedro harbor until the money was paid; that he would proceed against the captain criminally, and lose him his job; and that, in addition to all this, he would personally and singlehandedly beat hell out of him. This worked. Mr. and Mrs. Chapman took turns standing guard, twenty-four hours a day; they kept the cage packed in ice; they watched, fanned, and prayed; and after three weeks, they managed to get the animals to their home in Los Angeles.

What happened in the next three years sounds like something a movie writer would make up after spitting on his hands and really trying to please his producer. In the first place, the animals were all geared to the calendar as it works in the Andes, down under. They arrived in February, and thus had already begun to sprout the heavy fur that would enable them to endure the Andean winter when it begins in May. So in May, when Los Angeles gets hot, they came out in their new fur, and if you want to know how they felt for the next three months, just come out to Los Angeles in the summer time and begin to go around in a chinchilla coat. It took two years or so before Nature could get in step with the calendar, as we know it. Thus they were sickly; and what was worse, they wouldn't breed. This all checked up with what Mr. Chapman had been told by the Indians and others: it was impossible to raise these creatures in captivity.

Thus he was very gloomy, but then in another year they did begin to breed, and little ones appeared, and life took on a different color.

But then the menace, as the movie writer calls it, appeared, and caused plenty of grief. News of the experiment had got to Switzerland and a syndicate there subscribed a sum, placed it in the hands of an agent, and sent him to Mr. Chapman to buy animals for breeding in Switzerland, where it was thought the cold climate would suit them. Mr. Chapman, by now, had moved his stock to Tehachapi, in the California hills, and the appearance of the agent was his first realization that he had got hold of something that was commercially important. So he did some figuring. He found that no amount the agent could possibly pay would yield him as much as the animals themselves, later on, and he so refused to sell, at any price. The agent was in a hole, and he got out of it his own way. He stole the animals, instead of buying them. Mr. Chapman then had about seventy, and this man took half of them.

The ensuing chase led across a continent and an ocean, and Mr. Chapman's detectives finally located the animals in Germany. You see, on thinking it over, the agent thought it would be a good idea, since he had been so successful stealing the animals, to steal the money too, so he didn't go back to Switzerland at all. After various delays, the German courts decided in favor of Mr. Chapman, and the animals were returned to his representatives. But he never saw them again, for a cruel consideration intervened. He had pictures of the animals sent to him in California, and saw at once that they had been badly cared for and were ill. They had changed so in appearance that he couldn't positively identify them; thus, if he used them for breeding, they would cast a cloud on the pedigree of his whole stock, and as pedigree is all important to any breeder of animals, he had regretfully to renounce them and carry on with the animals that had been left to him by the thief, less than forty in number.

The forty, though, were enough, and now, from the original eleven brought from Chile, there are some five hundred pairs in the United States, of which four hundred are on Chapman's farm. Mr. Chapman died two years ago, but the venture is still being carried on by his son, R. E. Chapman. After the theft, the stock was moved to Inglewood, which is not so isolated. Not a single animal, by the way, has been killed so far for its pelt. No breeder could afford to. One raw chinchilla skin today brings about $85. A pair of breeders, alive, are worth $3,200, this being the price the Chapman farm asks and gets. Buyers, so far, have been chiefly fur syndicates, which have established farms at three or four places in the West, and raise their animals with success.

The farm itself is a small place of two or three acres, on which are rows and rows of neat cages. The cage is made of fine wire, to keep out snakes, rats and other pests. In each cage is a little house, with a small tunnel running up the side, leading inside. The animals live in the houses by day, and do not come out into the cages until night, as they are nocturnal. They are monogamous, and a pair once mated share the same cage for the rest of their lives. One to four babies are produced at a time. They are born with their eyes open, and within an hour of their birth are up and running around. The mother nurses them, and mother and father take turns at keeping an eye on them.

The farm operates on a strictly supervised schedule, with everything done at its own particular time, and every detail in connection with the animals entered on a record. Food is weighed or accurately measured. The diet consists of a handful of corn, about the same amount of oatmeal, a little lettuce, a little hay, a raw carrot or two, with now and then some special preparation. The cages are built with a layer of insulation compound between thin boards of wood, not to protect the animals from cold, but to protect them from heat. The idea is to make the cages cool in summer. There is an operating room shinier than the operating rooms of most hospitals, and a veterinarian comes down for surgery whenever there is trouble.

The venture is highly profitable, and still a long way from its peak. That is, it will still be a good many years before a pelt will be worth as much as a live animal, and furriers can get as many skins as they want.

I wish to say this to the model in New York: No, there's nothing *else* that I want to look at. I want a chinchilla coat, and wind, weather and Mr. Chapman permitting, my wife is going to have one—eventually.

*McCalls*
March, 1937

# Where the Wild Things Are

This is about the Wildlife Preserve at Largo, near Upper Marlboro in Prince George's County, as improbable a tale as ever was told to me, and I know no better place to begin that at its improbable beginning. Set up your cameras, then in Texas, on quite a goodlooking number, a blonde type girl, now exactly 10, but two years ago, when this whole thing started, 8. I don't name her, and won't name her father, either, for security reasons—not national, which are largely imaginary, but personal, which are real, but really real. I'll call her Femme Fatale, Femme for short, and simply call him Tex. So, Femme went to the circus one day, to Ringling Brothers and Barnum & Bailey combined shows, and fell hard for a dog, a white Spitz, who could walk on his hind legs, throw a back handspring, and roll over and play dead. Coming home, she announced she wanted one like it for Christmas. As this was mid-November, that left the time fairly short, but Tex called the circus and talked to the trainers, two brothers originally from Ireland, who were most cooperative, saying there'd be no trouble about it, except they couldn't deliver by Christmas. This was explained to Femme, who graciously granted a reprieve, and the brothers went to work.

Then, the next summer, they called with the news they had the dog, all trained and ready, and where should they bring him? Tex invited them out to the house, and they came but the dog did the conquering. He completely enchanted them all, especially Femme, as soon as she learned how to cue him, and things became quite sociable. The brothers told their personal history, how they'd had an animal farm, within a few miles of Dublin, before signing on with the Ringlings, and then, suddenly, they propositioned their host: Why didn't he start such a farm? They knew the perfect place, some land up in Maryland, which happened to be for sale. So Tex allowed as how he could think of no reason why not. Almost anyone else could have, but Tex for some reason couldn't—well don't blame me, I said the tale was improbable. So they all traipsed up to Maryland, had a look at the farm, and Tex bought it, or at least 400 acres of it, for a bit more than $1,000,000. Texas, you know—they do it big down there.

Then he got busy on things that had to be done, or rather, his righthand man got busy, one William Natter, who was brought in from

Texas. First, there was the matter of zoning, which none may escape in Prince George's. Originally, when Tex bought in, the place was Rural Residential, but an animal farm was quite special, and modifications had to be granted. So all sorts of hearings were held, and in the end a Special Exception Use clause was granted, letting the animals in, as well as spectators in their cars—this was to be a "drive through" animal farm. Then the Washington Suburban Sanitary Commission had to be petitioned, for a suitable sewer connection, and also a water supply. Then when all this was out of the way, blueprints had to be drawn, for fences, buildings, and roads, but Bill Natter cracked his whip, and there they were.

At this point, Tex got a case of cold feet. It occurred to him that if an orangoutan and a gibbon came hand-and-hand into this office, he wouldn't know which was which. It occurred to him he didn't know what a kudu ate. It occurred to him that perhaps he'd bitten off more than he could chew. So, we all know what terrible plays God writes in a case like that, with the repossess man claiming blood, the bank calling in loans, and the tears splashing down, at night. Not when He writes one for Texas. Because Tex no sooner began holding his feet to the fire than a buyer popped up from nowhere, and made him a very nice offer.

This smiling apparition was the American Broadcasting Company, which just happened to have a branch, the Scenic and Wildlife Attractions, that was already in the business, and asked nothing better than to take Tex's place off his hands. They had one wildlife place, for animals, at Silver Springs, down in Florida, and another for humans, if that's what they are, Weeki-Wachee, pronounced Wicky-Wacky, also in Florida—this last a mermaid ballet, performed under water, the girls swimming upside down in unison, doing the trudgen, in unison, and wobbling their bottoms in unison, like Charo. Why a broadcasting company has a mermaid ballet, that I have no idea, but I said improbable didn't I? So I didn't say *how* improbable.

Then, very

Make it very, very.

So ABC took over, lock stock, and barrel, including Bill Natter, and Tex bowed out, complete. Bill resumed where he'd left off, before being interrupted, now working for ABC, as Vice President and General Manager, and soon acquired an assistant, Michael T. Donahoe, as Director of Marketing. Between the two of them, they completely transformed the blueprints into wood, wire, and concrete, putting up buildings for the animals in winter, roads for the patrons to drive on, and fences to keep the animals from eating each other. And, of course, they had to get animals. How you get animals is (1) Catch them and bring 'em back alive by going on safari in Africa, or (2) Buy them, from zoos that are overstocked, circuses that have some they want to get rid of, for one reason and another, and places that breed them for sale. Mike Donahoe didn't take off for Africa, but he did visit the zoos, circuses, and breeding farms, coming up with quite a collection, which began to arrive by truck—not quietly, but at least alive and in good condition. At last things were ready, and after a party for bigwigs and press, Bill could announce the opening date, July 15.

So he opened.

Which is where I come in. It so happens I'm under obligation to a family down the street, the Younisses—not only to Dorothy and Jim, for hauling me around in their beautiful car, since I don't drive any more, but to all four children too, Carrie, Andy, Jessica, and Emily, who drop in all the time, pretendedly to say hello, actually to see if I have errands I'd like them to do. Naturally, I'm on the alert for ways to show my appreciation. So, reading about this opening, I called up and suggested we all have lunch, and then go visit the animals. Jim couldn't make it, but the rest accepted enthusiastically, and so one day we set off, Dorothy driving, me on the front seat beside her, the kids in back, clicking cartidges into a camera. But at lunch there came a diversion, in the shape of laughter, which would be suppressed, and then burst out again. The reason, it turned out, was the look on my face as I surveyed this world of the dog-on-a-bun, which I didn't really believe, even after I'd seen it—if I went into detail about it, you wouldn't believe it either, so we'll call it one more improbable thing. But to get their minds off me and the way I looked, Dorothy would advert to the Wildlife Preserve, telling them: "Now, don't expect too much."

"That's right," I would say, "remember, the place is new."

"It's only been open a month," Dorothy would say.

"Rome wasn't built in a day."

Her admonitions seemed to be sincere, and certainly mine were. What I expected I don't exactly know: something dusty, I think, like the old-time circus lot, before the arenas took over, with elephants, horses, and roustabouts churning the grass into clods, and pipes sticking out of the ground, with spigots on them, for water. So what I actually saw, as I waited for my change, buying tickets there at the gate, caused me utter astonishment. Far from being dusty, or scuffed out, or new, this was one of the most beautiful scapes I had ever seen, and had obviously been many years in the making. To the right, a short distance off the road, call it 50 yards, was a grove of verdant trees, some of them young and apparently planted, some of them very old, as they were gigantic. This grove wound off in the distance, and presently I saw that it followed a brook, a sparkling thing that burbled—sometimes so loud we could hear it. The name of the brook, I learned later, is Northeast Branch, but what it's a branch of I'm not quite sure I know, the Patuxent River, I think. To the left of the road, were gentle, rolling hills, covered with bright green grass. The road itself was a ribbon of neat concrete, rising and falling with the hills.

So my mouth must have been hanging open, but that wasn't all that was happening, there in the Youniss car. For even as I stared spellbound, the giggles turned to gurgles, of honest, spellbound ecstasy. Because dead ahead of the car, grazing by the side of the road, were buffalo, live American bison, looking just as they do in the books. At once the camera was pointed, and pictures began to be shot. Suddenly, blocking our way, was an animal asleep in the road, a gigantic thing, as high as the hood of our car. It seemed odd, for buffalo aren't really too big, not as big as our regular cattle. "That's a yak," suddenly whispered Andy. "It was in the paper—they have one. They put him in with the bison so he wouldn't get lonely."

This was in the American section, and we went on, past deer, caribou, bear, wolves, and antelope, while the spell I was under, instead of wearing off, possessed me more and more, until I was literally entranced. I am no stranger to zoos, and in some of them, notably the one at San Diego, you feel that they lodge their guests quite acceptably. But in most, you feel a sense of guilt, that you share responsibility, if only by mute acceptance, for the way these creatures are penned up, so most of them are obvious psychiatric, as they fidget and fret and stamp, from boredom and lack of exercise. With me, the reaction is religious, and I make no concealment of it, whether in a zoo or when confronted of the average human notion of what we owe the animal kingdom. A zoo can be defended on various grounds, but what of the mutilations we inflict, often for no rational reason? For example, we have a dog, a Doberman, that we make a family pet of. The dog has a tail that he loves, that he's proud of, and wags on any provocation. So what do we do? We send this dog to the vet to have his tail chopped off, and not only that, but the ears that reflect every emotion he feels, we have cropped so they are pointed. And why? I have yet to meet the owner of a Doberman dog who could tell you why he had it done. As for shooting animals for "sport," I suffer at the thought of it. As far as I'm concerned, these are beings created by God, with rights we ought to respect, but all too often don't.

Beyond the American section was the South American, with llamas, alpacas, and vicunas, but no jaguars. It turned out that while spotted cats in cages set up no safety problem, spotted cats in the open are different. For a jaguar can take a ten-foot fence at one bound, and can probably jump 14 feet. A 14-foot fence is expensive, and if it isn't quite jump-proof, a 16-foot fence mightn't be, for the reason that an ambitious jaguar might hook on at the ten-foot level, and go clambering up and over. Where he would wind up then, is too frightening to imagine—out on the highway, probably, with his eyes reflecting the headlights, and ladies screaming. Well I think I would scream too, for my religious feeling about him doesn't include a desire to be eaten. So, no spotted cats at Largo.

After the South Ameican section came the African, with zebras, rhinoceros, hyenas, giraffes, lions, and elephants, and plenty of them. The giraffes looked as they do on film, wild, in Africa—standing beside trees, their heads among the branches, munching leaves. They looked to be beautifully conditioned. The zebras were grazing, and a hyena, while we looked, actually laughed, or at any rate skinned back his lips in the hyena's not-too-mirthful grin. When we got to the lions we were held up two or three minutes by the car ahead of us, but then suddenly were face to face with a pack, or pride as they seem to be called. Two or three males studied us, lying down, and then suddenly came up on all fours. I confess I didn't much like it. "If we weren't in this car," I heard myself say, "I can't think of anything that would make me more nervous than a dozen lions taking an interest in us."

"I can," said Andy.

". . . Yeah? Like what?"

"*Two* dozen of 'em," said Andy.

He pointed, and sure enough, around a bend, were another bunch, also taking an interest. The giggles broke out again.

Further on, around a couple of bends, we came on a herd of

elephants, five or six adults and six or seven little ones. In our car, the babies were greeted with squeals, and indeed there's nothing quite so irresistible as a baby elephant, and nothing quite so mischievous. As Dorothy stopped, we all sat watching, while two of them chased each other and the big ones amiably paid no attention. But then suddenly we faced a situation. The biggest one of the adults, a female apparently, as it had no tusks, stepped out on the road and blocked us. Dorothy did nothing—she didn't spin her motor and didn't blow her horn. The elephant looked us in the eye. Then she stepped up and began polishing our lights with her trunk—first the light on the right hand side, then the one on the left. "Her name is Topsy," whispered Carrie. "It was in the paper about her. She was with Ringling Brothers circus, but was too contrary, and so they had to get rid of her."

"She wouldn't tail-up right," whispered Emily. "She kept lousing their exit, when the whole bunch finished their act."

"My but she's big," whispered Jessica.

"You—*git*," commanded Andy.

Topsy left off with the light and raised her head. At this moment a little one, squealing, ran under her, rubbing its back on her stomach. Amiably she followed it off, and Dorothy rolled us on. Well, if having your lights shined by an elephant isn't improbable, I don't really know what is.

That's about all. If you have a taste for such things, it's about as perfect of its kind as anything you're likely to see, and I commend it to you unreservedly—oh, I almost forget. They do have a kudu, so happens—which turns out to be an antelope, with fore and aft stripes and corkscrew horns. And if *that* isn't an improbability—!

*The Washington Post Potomac*
April 13, 1975

# The Raccoon

There's trouble in Prince George's County—so much trouble, and so bad, that I hate to start telling about it. So why don't I lead off with something good—like, let us say, Prince George's County weather, which I'm quite fanatic about, and regard as the county's biggest asset. For example, as I sit here in my Hyattsville home, writing away with my ballpoint, the second blizzard of the season is coming down outside, as it's been coming down all night. And yet Edward Kisielnicki, who lives next door and has the snow removal contract, hasn't got his shovel, or made preparations of any kind. The reason is that this blizzard, like the one three weeks ago and the five a year ago, is running off as rain, and will give no further trouble.

Such is the salubrious nature of Prince George's climate that when a blizzard does arrive, the air is balmy enough to forestall its freezing as flakes and ensure its descent as liquid—at a great saving of money, for snow, leave us face it, is costly. This agreeable state of affairs, of course, is most important commercially, especially to the county's main business, which at the moment is real estate.

Lucky Baldwin, the adventurer who developed the area around what is now the Santa Anita Racetrack, in California, when told that people complained of what he charged for the land, exclaimed: "The land? Prince George's is selling climate. Hell, we give the land away! We're selling climate!"

Prince George's is selling climate that's never too hot in summer or freezing cold in winter.

Prince George's is selling climate with moderate storms, whose lightning is far away and whose wind is of easy intensity.

Prince George's is selling climate that gives the first taste of Dixie—and indeed, as the top county of Southern Maryland's five, could be called The Gateway to Dixie.

So I spread the news around.

I first noticed the difference between Prince George's weather and other Maryland weather one night some years ago, just after I moved in from California, when some people from the Middle West, visiting friends in Chevy Chase, came to dinner with me at Harvey's, at the old Connecticut Avenue location. Dinner over, I rode them out to the house. But around eleven o'clock, happening to look out, I saw a powdering of snow on the ground, and hinted they should be running along. I supposed they would call a cab, but when they made no move to the phone I loaded them into the car once more and started out for Chevy Chase. But every mile saw deeper snow, until, by the time I got to the house they were staying at, I was plowing through six inches of it, and terrified that if their farewells were protracted much longer, I might be stuck there for the night, unable to move at all. However, I managed somehow to get back, but when I arrived back in Hyattsville, there was still barely an inch of snow in my drive.

After that, I began noticing the weather more, for example calling the year 1950 "the year without a summer," as in Prince George's through July it was spring, and beginning with August, autumn. And I began making comparisons, with the summer I spent in Charles County, where the continuous poker game in the back room of Robey's saloon had to suspend, as the players shed coats, shirts, and even undershirts, fingering their cards in exhaution; with the summer I spent in Washington, at that time paved with "asphalt," which became so soft in the heat that your heels sank down in it, and then lifted with black strings dangling down; with the winter I spent in Montgomery, where the snow was so deep and the cold so intense that no traffic moved on the roads, and to get to the District for a weekend I had to slog down in rubber boots to the Germantown station, and change to shoes in my hotel room. Piecing these bits of evidence together, along with other things I noted, I began to wonder if bad weather in various places wasn't due in large part to the rivers that flow past their shores, and if good weather in other places wasn't due to the absence of the rivers that act as conduits to storms, heat waves, and cold cold pockets. I remembered suddenly my father's prognostications before storms that came up, or didn't come up, perhaps, after threatening.

My father fancied himself an economist, and was one I have to admit, but what he knew definitively was football, and even more than that weather. In Chestertown, where he lived while he was president of the college, he would go out to the tennis courts, have a look at the clouds, and usually announce: "This'll be mostly wind,"—and so it would always turn out. But sometimes he would suddenly start for the house, legging it fast, taking long steps, and tell me: "Let's get those windows down—this is going to be bad." In Chestertown, bad meant really bad. The Chester is an asset worth millions and millions and millions to the town—it is wide, deep, and clean, and most important of all, free of the nettles that curse the Bay. And so it has become a vacation paradise, with mansions lining its banks, owned mostly by residents of Wilmington, Del., that financial hub of the universe. But when it acts as a storm conduit, the results can be fantastically frightening. It figured, along with another river nearby, in my father's prognostications, as I learned, little by little. If the look of the clouds told him the storm would follow the Sassafras, some miles to the north, down into the Bay, he would know we would get the edges, but no more. If it was going to follow the Chester, however, he would know we'd better get to the windows, and get to them fast.

So, I've come to believe that rivers, such blessings in many ways, are not blessings at all, when it comes to their effect on weather. Places like New York, Philadelphia, and Washington, all on broad, deep rivers, are also, by a funny coincidence, cursed with horribly hot summers, frighteningly cold winters, and storms of malignant intensity. And of course the Father of Waters, our beautiful Mississippi, with its tremendous tributaries, the Missouri, Ohio, Arkansas, and Cumberland, to mention just a few, is also the father of the most fanatically horrible weather known on the face of this earth. I remember staggering off the plane one night in pajamas, at Kansas City, Mo., while the stewardess sicced her finger at me, just to get a breath of air in the stifling heat, which surpassed anything I'd ever known. And of course, the rivers bless this whole area with a feature not seen elsewhere, tornadoes.

I could go on and on, as I think of the heat waves we don't get, while Washington swelters in them, and the cold waves we don't get either, and the snow we don't get, and all the rest of it. I have no doubt Mr. Kelly, our up-and-coming County Executive, wishes I would, and I would ask nothing better than to accommodate him. But, so far as this piece goes, I've about run out the string, and had better get on to what I started to talk about. All is not hotsy or even totsy in Prince George's County. Calamity hath struck, a speck is there in the ointment, a fly swims around in the soup: we have a raccoon invasion. Yes, I said, raccoon—that animal which figured so big in the news a few years ago, when E. H. Crump of Memphis, Boss Crump, known as, said Estes Kefauver reminded him of one, "looking at you with that honest expression, and all the time with his paw in the bureau drawer, feeling around for what he can steal." So Kefauver came out in a coonskin hat, and that settled Boss Crump's hash, but did little for a raccoon's image. At the time, I thought it a bit of a libel on a harmless but handsome animal, and one known for its friendly ways. I've now come to the conclusion that Boss Crump's description was flattery. They are, leave us face it, a God-awful pest. They're all over the place, even my place. They've cut a hole in my back screen, are on my back porch every night, scattering refuse around in an indescribably messy way. My neighbors make the same report—Keith Dunklee, up the street, looked out the other night, to find four of them looking at *him*. The reason for the plague nobody knows, but most people think it's related to the trash-liner bag. This is comparatively recent, and in some ways a big improvement over the system we used to have. Formerly we put it in cans that we lined with newspaper, for the men to take to their truck, empty, and bring back. But all this was considerable trouble, and the cans every so often had to be rinsed with hot water mixed with cleaning fluid, a bit of a job. So the trash-liner bag, which goes in a hamper hung by three clothes-pins, simplified everything. The night before collection, we lift the bag out of the hamper, close it with the tabs it has on the edge, and leave it for the men. They take it to the truck and pitch it in, where it goes into the mangle, bag and all. There's no can to be brought back, no scald job later on, no anything troublesome. The whole procedure is simplified, and of course quite a lot cheaper, as fewer men are required on the truck.

So improvement was marked, except that these bags are duck soup to raccoons. The old can they could rarely get into, but the trash liner bag presents them no problem at all. And what to do about them nobody has any idea. The first thing anyone thinks of, of course, is poison, but this is easier thought of than used. To begin with, it might be successful and kill some raccoons, but also might kill the neighbor's beloved cat, which wouldn't be so good. Also, even assuming considerable success, four or five dead raccoons out there in the morning, would present a problem of a very critical kind. Also, any plan for killing them runs into something else: their charm, that Boss Crump alluded to. Harry Piper ran into this, and it made an impression on him. He's on the faculty at the University, and often works late getting ready for classes next day. So one night, hearing something outside, he opened the back door to find a raccoon out there, staring up at him in an unmistakably friendly way. "Obviously it wanted in," says Harry, "and I had an impulse to invite him. Actually, I shooed him off, but the whole thing was a bit bewildering." Another night, he and Alice heard something topside, went out, and found a raccoon in the chimney, hanging on with forepaws, hind legs dangling down. It was keeping warm, apparently. They threw things at it and presently frightened it off, but were horrified for some minutes lest it slip and bang down on the fire. A singed raccoon, charging around the living room and howling, wasn't their idea of a nice end for an evening.

I wrote that far last night, reserving for today my finish, which would be a plea to all and sundry, in case you're contemplating a move to Prince George's, not to be put off by a few harmless raccoons. I was going to predict that the bag manufacturers will come up with something soon, possibly a see-through plastic drum with snap-on top, which can hold the bag overnight, for the men in the morning. I expected to say this, and do. But during the night something happened that I think also wants saying. I watched Merv Griffin on TV, then had a mug of icewater, then went out in the kitchen to close up and make ready for bed. Like Harry Piper I heard something outside. Opening the door I saw a shadow in one corner of the porch, that seemed to move. Getting a flashlight from the dining room, I armed it, and sure enough eyes were staring at me out of dark stripes across a face. Just beyond was a tail with black-and-white rings. I came back inside and sat down to think.

Checking back on the day's menu, I realized it had included nothing to tempt a raccoon, which the encyclopedia had said is carniverous. So presently I went to the refrig and took out my bowl of ham. The Pantry, my market, bones the ham for me and puts it on their slicer, so I can make sandwiches of it for lunch in the afternoon. But the slices are quite large, with outer borders I don't have to have. So I peeled off a few of these, cut them up with the snips, and put them in a bowl. Then I went out on the back porch and put the bowl down. "Hey," I called. "You, I'm talking to! Come and get it, now is no time to be bashful."

You'd be surprised at the action that got. In two, no more than three darts, my visitor was there, his nose down in the bowl, eating his ham fricasee. I reached over and gave him a pat. He responded, very friendly, by raising his head for a moment, before going back to the ham. Remembering that ham is quite salty, I went back, filled another bowl with water, went out, and put it beside the first. He sniffed it, lapped it a moment or two, then went back to the ham. When he finished it up, I took both bowls back in the kitchen, washed

them and put them away. When I went back, he had vanished.
He'll be back, I don't have to be told.
God save me, I now have a pet raccoon.

*The Washington Post*
February 15, 1976

# Crime and Punishment

The other day I saw a friend of mine knock her offspring ten feet, and it set me to thinking. The lady is a lioness, and the young article's offense consisted of repeatedly, wilfully and maliciously playing with her tail, in spite of several warnings to stop. Then he got it in the puss. And then he stopped.

Here, it seemed to me, was revealed the true nature of punishment, more clearly than in a dozen books. This cub wasn't being given something unpleasant, measured out carefully in return for something forbidden. It was much simpler than that. It was a plain establishment of superiority, a showdown on whether he was running that cage or mamma was running it. That is what punishment is, I think, in the average home, and it shows why impudence, with its first cousin, wilful disobedience, is the most heinous crime a child can commit, and the only crime for which most children ever get spanked.

But I suspect the principle applies to more than lion cubs and children. I think it applies to the criminal himself, and that neglect of it is what has got modern penology into such a morass of theories. As our prison boards flounder between the ancient theory of retributive justice, and the newer theory of exemplary justice, and the still newer theory of reformative justice, they are constantly guilty of undue harshness on the one hand and undue leniency on the other, and still crime goes on unchecked. What they leave out of account is this thing which a lioness, or a parent, or the policeman who gives the thug a dose of the nightstick before bringing him in, understands very well and instinctively—that what you are really trying to do is show who is running the country, the criminal or the law. In other words, you are establishing superiority.

But at present there is no establishment of superiority, and you get the basis for the average man's belief that what counts is not the severity of punishment but its speed and certainty. Suppose the lioness had had to struggle with that cub, would that have established superiority? It would not. He would have felt that he had given her such a battle that the next time he would probably win.

So with modern criminal procedure. It is true that after stealing the watch a criminal often goes to jail. But if it takes a year to send him there, if his lawyer keeps him out on bail, wins postponements, hangs a jury or two, and he almost beats the rap, then he is contumacious, and feels that next time he can get off scot free. And, alas, he is probably right.

Stealing is stealing. Stealing second base, many get thrown out, but the decision is close, and somebody always takes a chance. But in stealing home base they get thrown out by ten feet, and nobody takes a chance. That is what we need; to throw the criminal out by ten feet, so his face is red, and he knows he was a fool. That, of course, leads to courts and their badly needed reformation. I would like to see my friend the lioness preside over one for a day. I think it would get reformed pretty quick.

Hearst column
January 8, 1934